East India Company

Copies of the Several Testimonials Transmitted from Bengal

By the Governor General and Council, Relative to Warren Hastings

East India Company

Copies of the Several Testimonials Transmitted from Bengal
By the Governor General and Council, Relative to Warren Hastings

ISBN/EAN: 9783337186142

Printed in Europe, USA, Canada, Australia, Japan

Cover: Foto ©Suzi / pixelio.de

More available books at **www.hansebooks.com**

C O P I E S

OF THE

SEVERAL TESTIMONIALS

TRANSMITTED FROM BENGAL

BY THE

GOVERNOR GENERAL AND COUNCIL,

RELATIVE TO

WARREN HASTINGS, Esq.

LATE GOVERNOR GENERAL OF BENGAL.

LONDON:

PRINTED FOR JOHN STOCKDALE, OPPOSITE
BURLINGTON-HOUSE, PICCADILLY.

M DCC LXXXIX.

ADVERTISEMENT.

THE Editor fuppofed that it would fwell the prefent Publication unneceffarily, if the Names of all the Perfons were printed who have figned the Addreffes. He has, therefore, contented himfelf with a general Defcription of the perfons who fign each Addrefs, except in a few Inftances.

June 25, 1789.

A 2

Extract of General Letter from Bengal, dated 6th November 1788, received by the Ship William Pitt; and of General Letter from Bengal, dated 9th January 1789, received by the Kent, tranfmitting the following Papers, accompanied with the original Perfian Addreffes to the Court of Directors.

Extract of General Letter from Bengal, dated 6th November 1788.

Par. 309. FOUR feveral Addreffes from the principal Native Inhabitants of Benares, to your Honourable Court, declaring their Sentiments of Mr. Haftings, were fubmitted to us by Mr. George Thompfon, late Secretary to Mr. Haftings, at the Requeft of Ally Ibrahim Cawn, the Chief Judicial Magiftrate of that City, with the Correfpondence which had paffed with him on the Subject of them.

310. It appeared from the Tenor of this Correfpondence, that a Deputation of the Inhabitants of Benares had expreffed their Wifhes, through Ally Ibrahim Cawn, to wait upon your Refident Mr. Duncan with thefe Addreffes, as the regular official Channel of Communication; but that Mr. Duncan had declared it was unneceffary

ceſſary for the Inhabitants to attend him with the Addreſſes, as they did not concern the Company's Affairs.—Under theſe Circumſtances they were forwarded to Mr. Thompſon, as the Attorney and Friend of Mr. Haſtings, with a Requeſt that he would lay them before the Governor General in Council, and take the neceſſary Steps for their being tranſlated and tranſmitted to Europe.

311. In compliance with Ally Ibrahim Cawn's Solicitation, Mr. Thompſon ſubmitted theſe Papers to us, as before recited, requeſting that they might be tranſlated and forwarded to you in due Time ; and under a Suppoſition that the Company would not be averſe to receive from its Native Subjects and Allies, the public Declaration of their Sentiments, upon a Queſtion of ſo much Importance to their Happineſs, and to the Credit of the Engliſh Nation, as the Conduct of Mr. Haſtings, during his long Government, Mr. Thompſon further, requeſted, that he might be permitted to receive the Suffrages which the Native Inhabitants of the Company's Poſſeſſions were deſirous of conveying to the Court of Directors, as their Senſe of Mr. Haſtings's Merits ; and that the Judges, Collectors, and Reſidents might be informed that he had obtained ſuch Permiſſion, or that they were themſelves at liberty to receive and tranſmit to us any Teſtimonies relative to Mr. Haſtings, that might be tendered to them by or on the Part of the Native Inhabitants.

312. With theſe Requeſts from Mr. Thompſon we complied, having qualified our Orders to the Judges, Collectors, and Reſidents, in the following Terms : " That the Liberty accorded
" was

" was merely to receive and tranfmit Teftimo-
" nials when offered ; but that they were not
" to deduce any Inference from it, that they
" were authorifed to exercife any further Inter-
" ference."

313. The Addreffes above mentioned, with
Tranflations, and various other Addreffes, &c.
from the Nabob Vizier and his Minifters, from
the Nabobs of Furruckabad, and thefe Provinces, alfo from the principal Zemindars of
Dinagepore, Boglepore, &c. &c. &c. according to a Lift which accompanies them, attend
you in the prefent Difpatch.

*Extract of General Letter from Bengal, dated the
9th January* 1789.

Par. 20. Several further Addreffes, refpecting
Mr. Haftings, which were either forwarded by
the Collectors, or prefented by Native Vackeels,
to the Governor General, having been tranflated
purfuant to our Orders, are now tranfmitted in
the Packet of the Kent.—We alfo forward an Addrefs from the Greeks, with a Tranflation of it.

Copy of a Letter from Mr. Thompfon,
dated 27th March 1788.

To Earl Cornwallis, K. G. Governor General, &c.

Fort William, 27th March 1788.

My Lord,

THE principal Native Inhabitants of Benares
having in Four feveral Addreffes to the
Honourable Company declared their Sentiments
of

of Mr. Haſtings, were deſirous of delivering the Addreſſes to Mr. Duncan, the Reſident at that Place, in order that he might forward them to the Governor General in Council, and that they might be ſo tranſmitted to the Court of Directors. To this End, Ally Ibrahim Khawn, the Chief Judicial Magiſtrate at Benares, wrote to Mr. Duncan, requeſting that he would appoint a Time when a Deputation of the Inhabitants might attend him with the Addreſſes: Mr. Duncan returned for Anſwer to Ally Ibrahim Khawn, that as the Addreſſes did not concern the Company's Affairs, it was unneceſſary that the Inhabitants ſhould either come or ſend to him; under theſe Circumſtances, Ally Ibrahim Khawn, at the Inſtance of the Parties who had ſigned the Addreſſes, forwarded them to me, in order that I might preſent them to the Governor General in Council, for the purpoſe of being tranſmitted to England.

The Circumſtances, as I have here ſtated them, will appear from Ally Ibrahim Khawn's Letter to Mr. Duncan's Anſwer, and Ally Ibrahim Khawn's Letter to me, Copies and Tranſlations of which I take the liberty of encloſing, Nº 1.

In compliance with the Requiſition which I have thus received, I have now the Honour to lay before your Lordſhip the ſeveral Perſian Papers mentioned in the encloſed Liſt, Nº 2; and as well on the Part of the Native Inhabitants of Benares as of Mr. Haſtings, moſt earneſtly to requeſt that your Lordſhip will be pleaſed to order that the ſaid Perſian Papers may be tranſlated into Engliſh by the proper Officers, and with

the

the Tranflations tranfmitted to the Court of Directors by the next Ship.

As I humbly conceive that the Honourable
Company will not be averfe to receiving from
its Native Subjects and Allies the Public Declaration of their Sentiments upon a Queftion of fo
much Importance to their Happinefs, and to the
Credit of the Englifh Nation, as the Conduct of
Mr. Haftings during his long Government ; and
as I underftand that the principal Native Inhabitants throughout the Company's Poffeffions
are defirous of conveying to the Court of Directors their Senfe of Mr. Haftings's Merits, I
take the liberty of requefting that I may be permitted to receive their Suffrages, and that the
Gentlemen who act as Judges, Collectors, or Refidents under the Prefidency of Fort William,
may be officially informed that I have obtained
fuch Permiffion, and that they have Authority to
tranfmit to the Governor General in Council any
Teftimonies relative to Mr. Haftings, which
may be tendered to them for that Purpofe, by
or on the Part of the Native Inhabitants of their
refpective Diftricts.

> I have the Honour to be,
>> My Lord,
>>> Your Lordfhip's
>>>> moft devoted and
>>>>> obedient humble Servant,

(Signed) GEO. NESBIT THOMPSON.

> (A true Copy.)
>> E. HAY,
>>> Sec^y to the Gov^t.

First Enclosure in Mr. Thompson's Letter.

Translation of a Letter from Ally Ibrahim Khawn, the Chief Judicial Magistrate at Benares, to Jonathan Duncan, Esquire, the Resident at that Place.

THE Inhabitants of this City have prepared, under their Seals and Signatures, several Addresses relative to the beneficent and honourable Mr. Hastings.—They wish to send to you certain Persons on their Part with the said Addresses, and to deliver to you a Petition to this Effect; viz. Be pleased, in your Kindness, to forward these Addresses to the Presence of the Right Honourable Earl Cornwallis, to whom be lasting Prosperity, and to the Honourable Gentlemen of his Council in Calcutta, who having graciously caused them to be translated by the Translators of the Company, will (it is requested) be pleased to forward them to the Honourable Directors in England, as has been already fully represented to you by Beneram Pundit. Whenever you shall be pleased to appoint, the said Persons will attend you, and present the said Address.

Translation of Mr. Duncan's Answer to Ally Ibrahim Khawn.

Usual Compliments.

Your Letter, informing me that the Inhabitants of the City have prepared, under their Seals and Signatures, several Addresses relative to Mr. Hastings, and are desirous that certain Persons should come to me with the said Addresses,

dreffes, and a Requeft that I will forward them
to his Lordfhip in Council; has been received.
As the Addreffes have no Connection with the
Bufinefs of the Company, there is no Neceffity
that they (the Inhabitants) fhould come or fend
to me. Let them do what they think proper.
What more ? &c.

*Tranflation of a Letter from Ally Ibrahim Khawn
to Mr. Thompfon.*

The ufual Compliments.

The Inhabitants of the Town of Benaris having prepared feveral Addreffes, under their Seals
and Signatures, relative to Mr. Haftings, were
defirous that certain of the Inhabitants fhould
carry the Addreffes, and deliver them to Mr.
Duncan, in order that he might in his Kindnefs
forward them to the Council in Calcutta, and requeft, in behalf of the Inhabitants, that the beneficent Gentlemen of the Council, having caufed the Addreffes to be tranflated by the Tranflator of the Company, the Centre of Profperity,
would fend both the Originals and the Tranflations to England, to the Prefence of the Honourable the Directors. I accordingly wrote to
Mr. Duncan; he fent for Anfwer, that as the
Addreffes had no Relation to the Bufinefs of the
Company, it was therefore unneceffary that they
(the Inhabitants) fhould come or fend to him —
This you will underftand from the Copies which
I fend enclofed of my Letter on this Occafion
to Mr. Duncan, and of his Anfwer. As you
are the Attorney and the Friend of Mr. Haftings, they have therefore fent the Addreffes to
you—They will be delivered to you by Mirza

Ally

Ally Nukky Khawn Behadre.—It is defired that you will deliver them to the Honourable the Gentlemen of the Council, and take fuch Steps that they may be tranflated and fent to England. What more ? &c.

(True Copies.)

E. HAY,
Secr^y to the Gov^t.

Second Enclofure in Mr. Thompfon's Letter.

ENCLOSURE, N° 2.

A. An Addrefs under the Seals of the Maha Rajah and Ranny, the Kawjies, Mufties, Mowlavies, Munfubdars, Khawns, and other Perfons of Diftinction at Benaris, bearing 277 Seals.

a. A Copy of the above Addrefs, with a Schedule fpecifying the Names, Offices, and Stations of the Perfons whofe Seals are affixed to the Addrefs. This Copy and Schedule are attefted by the Official Seal of the Kauzy Ally Nukky Khawn.

B. Addrefs under the Signatures of the Pundits of Mehrift and Naugur, and other Bramins at Benares, written in the Shanfcrit Language and in the Dio Nugry Character.

178 Signatures.

b. Copy of the above Addrefs, marked B. attefted by the Official Seal of the Kauzy.

C. An

C. An Addreſs in the Shanſcrit Language and in the Bengal Character, ſigned by the Bengal Pundits reſiding at Benares.
112 Signatures.

c. A Copy of the Addreſs marked C. atteſted by the Official Seal of the Kauzy.

D. Addreſs in the Hindoſtany Language and in the Guzarauty Character, ſigned by the Bankers of the Now Putty Quarter, the Merchants, &c. of Benares.
402 Signatures.

d. Copy of the above Addreſs marked D. atteſted by the Official Seal of the Kauzy.

(A true Copy.)
E. HAY,
Sec^y to the Govr.

Reſolutions of the Right Honourable the Governor General in Council, on Mr. Thompſon's Letter, 31ſt March 1788.

Reſolutions on Mr. Thompſon's Letter, in Conſultation 31ſt March 1788.

THE Governor General in Council, having conſidered the Requeſt made by Mr. Thompſon, does not conceive himſelf authoriſed to preclude Mr. Thompſon, as the Attorney to Mr. Haſtings, collecting the Suffrages of the Natives, or to reject an Application

3   founded

founded in common Juſtice, and therefore reſolves to admit it, ſo far as to authoriſe the Officers of Government to receive Repreſentations from the Natives, expreſſive of their Senſe of Mr. Haſtings's Conduct towards them, and to tranſmit them, if tendered, to the Secretary, with reſpect to theſe Teſtimonials.

The Governor General in Council deems it wholly unneceſſary to record any Opinion upon a Subject with which he has no Concern or Interference.

Ordered, That the following Circular Letters be written to the Collectors, Judges, and Reſidents.

Mr. Mathew Dawſon, Collector of Moorſhedabad.

Sir,

Mr. Thompſon, who appears to be one of Mr. Haſtings's Attorneys, underſtanding that the principal Native Inhabitants of the Company's Territories are deſirous of bearing Teſtimony to the Merits of Mr. Haſtings, has addreſſed the Governor General in Council, requeſting that he may be permitted to receive their Suffrages, and that the Judges, Collectors, or Reſidents under this Preſidency, may have Authority to tranſmit to the Governor General in Council any Teſtimonies relative to Mr. Haſtings, which may be tendered to them for that Purpoſe, by or on the Part of the Native Inhabitants of their reſpective Diſtricts; with this Requeſt the Governor General in Council has been pleaſed to comply; and I have therefore to inform you, that ſhould any ſuch Addreſſes be tendered to you by or on the Part of
the

the Native Inhabitants within your Diſtrict, you are at Liberty to receive and forward them to me. The Liberty now accorded is merely to receive and tranſmit Teſtimonials when offered; and you are not to deduce any Inference from it that you are authoriſed to exerciſe any further Interference in this Buſineſs.

I am, &c.

(Signed) E. HAY,
Secʸ to the Govᵗ.

31ſt March 1788.

The ſame to

Mr. Peter Speke   Collector of Rajeſhahy,
Mr. Suetonius Heatly   Dᵒ of Perneah,
Mr. Day Wᵗ M'Dowal Dᵒ of Rungpore,
Mr. Geo. Hatch   Dᵒ of Dinagepore,
Mr. Robᵗ Bathurſt   Dᵒ of Tirhoot,
Mr. Montgomiree   Dᵒ of Sircâr Sarum,
Mr. Wᵐ Brook   Dᵒ of Shawnbad,
Mr. Thomas Law   Dᵒ of Bahar,
Mr. Wᵐ Leſlie   Dᵒ of Ramghur,
Mr. Robᵗ Adair   Dᵒ of Boglepore,
Mr. J. Sherburn   Dᵒ of Beerbhoome,
Mr. J. Kenlock   Dᵒ of Burdwan,
Mr. Coſby Burrows   Dᵒ of Midnapore,
Mr. Wᵐ Pye   Dᵒ of 24 Pergunnahs,
Mr. Tightman Hinckle Dᵒ of Jeſſore,
Mr. Shearman Bird   Dᵒ of Chittagong,
Mr. Mathew Day   Dᵒof DaccaJelalpore,
Mr. Wᵐ Wroughton   Dᵒ of Momen Sing,
Mr. John Champain   Judge of Dacca,
Mr. Edᵈ Eyre Burgeſs   Dᵒ of Moorſhedabad,
Mr. Laurence Meun   Dᵒ of Patna,
Mr. Jonathan Duncan   Reſident at Benares.
C. Wᵐ Malet, Eſq.   Reſident at Poona.

Sir,

Mr. Thompson, who appears to be One of Mr. Hastings's Attornies, understanding that several of the principal Natives of India are desirous of bearing Testimony to the Merits of Mr. Hastings, has addressed the Governor General in Council, requesting that he may be permitted to receive their Suffrages, and that the Officers of Government may have Authority to transmit to the Governor General in Council any Testimonies relative to Mr. Hastings, which may be tendered to them for that Purpose by or on the Parts of the Natives of India.

With this Request the Governor General in Council has been pleased to comply ; and I have therefore to inform you, that should any such Addrefs be tendered to you, you are at liberty to receive and forward them to me. The Liberty now accorded is merely to receive and transmit Testimonials when voluntarily offered ; and you are not to deduce any Inference from it that you are authorised to exercise any further Interference in this Business.

I am, &c.

(Signed) E. HAY,

31st March 1788.   Secy to the Govt.

The same to Major Palmer, Resident with Mahajee Sindia, E. O. Ives, Esq. Resident at Lucknow.

Ordered that the Persian Papers, mentioned in Mr. Thompson's Enclosure, No 2, be translated into English by the Persian Translator, and transmitted to the Honourable Court of Directors with the Translations by the next Ship.

(A true Copy)

E. HAY, Secy to the Govt.

Copy of Three Letters from the Deputy
Perſian Tranſlator, accompanying Tranſlation of the different Teſtimonials re-
ſpecting Mr. Haſtings.

To Edward Hay, Eſquire, Secretary to the
Government.

Sir,

ACCOMPANYING I have the Pleaſure to
tranſmit you Tranſlations of ſeveral Addreſſes from his Excellency the Nawob Vizier
and principal Officers of his Court; from the
Rajah and reſpectable Inhabitants of Benares;
from the Nawob of Furruckabad, his Miniſters,
and Chief Merchants and Bankers of that City;
from the Nawob Mobarek ul Dowla, and the
principal Perſons of the Nizamut, and Cities of
Moorſhedabad and Rajemahl; and from the
Zemindar of Dinagepore and his Officers; which
I have made in purſuance to an Order from the
Governor General in Council, communicated to
me by you on the 27th April laſt.

Thoſe from Benares, Moorſhedabad, and Ra-
jemahl, ſent me by you (the latter Places accom-
panied by the Letter from the Reſident at the
Durbar), are in Duplicate in the Perſian Lan-
guage, as well as thoſe from Lucknow, with a
Letter from his Excellency the Vizier, to the
Governor General in Council. And I have the
Pleaſure to tranſmit you the Duplicates of the
Perſian, &c. Addreſſes, with the Tranſlations,
having compared them with their Counterparts,
which I have lodged among the Records of my
Office. Thoſe from Furruckabad and Dinage-

C   pore

pore I have copied, and, reserving the Copies
for the above Purpose, the Originals accompany
my present Address. The Letters from the
Vizier and Nawaub of Furruckabad, appertain-
ing to the Persian Office; and being addressed
to Earl Cornwallis, I have sent Persian Copies of
them attested.

All the above Papers are more particularly
described in the accompanying List.

Conceiving you would not want these Papers until near the Dispatch of the first Ship for
Europe, I have made the Translations when the
current and more urgent Business of my Office
would permit. This I hope will apologize for
the Delay.

I am, Sir,

Your most obedient Servant,

Calcutta,   (Signed)   G. F. CHERRY,
30th July 1788.   D. P. T'.

(A true Copy.)
E. Hay,
Sec'.

To Edward Hay, Esquire, Secretary to the
Government.

Sir,

Since I addressed you on the 30th July last,
I have received several other Addresses, of which
I have made Translations, agreeable to the Order
from the Governor General in Council, under
Date the 27th April last.

4   The

The accompanying Lift will point out the Particulars of the above Papers, being the Addreffes, with their Tranflations.

I am, Sir,

Your moft obedient Servant,

Calcutta, (Signed) G. F. CHERRY,

17th Sept. 1788. D. P. T'.

(A true Copy.)

E. Hay,

Sec'ʸ to the Gov'.

To Edward Hay, Efquire, Secretary to the Government.

Sir,

I have now the Pleafure to forward you further Teftimonials relative to Mr. Haftings, as per feparate accompanying Lift, with Tranflations of each.

The Letter from the Collector of Nudea will explain the Circumftance of the Seal of Rajah Seo Chund being affixed to an Addrefs from him, which was not delivered until after his Demife; and the Letters from the other Collectors, which accompanied the Addreffes from the Zemindars, &c. of their refpective Diftricts, were not fent to me,

I am, Sir,

Your moft obedient humble Servant,

(Signed) G. F. CHERRY,

Calcutta, D' P. T'.

4th Nov. 1788.

(A true Copy.)

E. Hay,

Sec' to the Gov'.

Copy Translation of Persian Address from Benares.

Translation of an Address marked A. under the Seals as under-written:

ALL we, residing, born, or on a Visit at Benares, whether of the Hindoo Religion, or Followers of Mahomet, have heard that the Gentlemen in England are displeased with Mr. Hastings, on Suspicion that he oppressed us Inhabitants of this Place, took our Money by Deceit and Force, and ruined the Country; therefore we, upon the Strength of our Religion and religious Tenets, which we hold as a Duty upon us, and in order to act conformable to the Decrees of God in delivering Evidence, relate the praiseworthy Actions, full of Prudence and Rectitude, Friendship and Politeness, of Mr. Hastings, possessed of great Abilities and Understanding; and by representing Facts, remove the Doubts that have possessed the Minds of the Gentlemen in England, that Mr. Hastings distributed Protection and Security to Religion, and Kindness and Peace to us all:—He is free from the Charge of Embezzlement and Fraud, and his Heart is void of Covetousness and Avidity; during the Period of his Government no one experienced from him other than Protection and Justice, never having felt Hardships from him, nor did the Poor ever know the Weight of an oppressive Hand from him. Our Characters and Reputations have been always guarded in Quiet from Attack by the Vigilance of his Prudence and Foresight, and

preserved

preserved by the Terror of his Juſtice. He never omitted the ſmalleſt Inſtance of Kindneſs and Goodneſs towards us and thoſe entitled to it, but always applied by Soothings and Mildneſs, the Salve of Comfort to the Wounds of Affliction, not allowing a ſingle Perſon to be overpowered by Deſpair.—He diſplayed his Friendſhip and Kindneſs to all.—He deſtroyed the Powers of Enemies and wicked Men by the Strength of his Terror.—He tied the Hands of Tyrants and Oppreſſors by his Juſtice, and by his Conduct he ſecured Happineſs and Joy to us.—He re-eſtabliſhed the Foundation of Juſtice; and we at all Times during his Government lived in Comfort, and paſſed our Days in Peace. —We are many many of us ſatisfied and pleaſed with him.—As Mr. Haſtings was perfectly well acquainted with the Manners and Cuſtoms of theſe Countries, he was always deſirous of performing that which would tend to the Preſervation of our Religion and of the Duties of our Sects, and guard the religious Cuſtoms of each from the Effects of Misfortunes and Accidents.—In every Senſe he treated us with Attention and Reſpect.—We have repreſented without Deceit what we have ourſelves ſeen, and the Facts that happened from him.

The Seals affixed to this Addreſs.

Seals of Caazees, - - - 6
Of Muftis, - - - 7
Of Learned Men, - - - 12
Of Men of Family, and holding Offices, 45
Of the Rajah and his Family, - - 19
_____
Carried over 89

Brought over   89
Seals of Mahomedan Inhabitants and
  Refidents in Benares, - - - 67
Of refpe&ctable Hindoo Inhabitants, - - 33
Of thofe who enjoy Penfions and Allow-
  ances, - - - - - 89

Total Seals,   278

Tranflation of a Paper marked B.

The Perfian Tranflation of a Paper, written
by the Maharatta Nagur, and every other Set
of Pundits and Bramins, under their Signatures,
in the Shanfcrit Language and Deonagur Characters.——" We, who are Inhabitants and Refidents in the Country and City of Benares, declare, That we are pleafed and fatisfied with the
Condu&ct and Kindnefs of Mr. Haftings ;—ift,
for his Exertions for the Profperity of Caafhy
(Benaris), the Refidence of Bifhefherjee, and the
principal Place of Worfhip of all the Hindoos of
Hindoftan.—2dly, For the Eafe and Credit we
experienced during his Government.—3dly,
Becaufe formerly there were great Oppreffions
committed by Gunga Puthan (Brahmins who
officiate in the Duties of Religion) on the Pilgrims ; on which Account few Pilgrims came:
Thefe be removed, and confequently the Number of Pilgrims is now increafed from all Parts
of Hindoftan : This Treatment was never before
experienced.—4thly, He appointed the Nawaub
Ally Ibrahim Cawn for the Prote&ction and Adminiftration of Juftice in this City, becaufe this
Magiftrate poffeffed Abilities, is juft and difin-
terefted.

terefted. He inferted in the Regulations delivered to him, that the Decifion of Difputes between Hindoos or Mahomedans muft be made
according to their refpective religious Tenets.
If Mahomedans, according to the Rites of
Iflam: And nominated learned Men to expound
the Laws of the Khoran. If Hindoos, agreeable
to the Shaftah: And appointed Pundits to lay
down the Rules of it. And he alfo provided in
the Regulations for the Peace and Quiet of us.
This Magiftrate exerts himfelf for our Peace,
and has ftopt all Taxes, Bribery, or other Ex-
pence, during his Adminiftration; and we
enjoy, during his Adminiftration, more Quiet
than during thofe of Rajah Bulwant Sing and
Rajah Cheyte Sing.—5thly, That during the
Time he refided in Benaris, Mr. Haftings treated
us all, on a Vifit to him, with Kindnefs and
Refpect, according to the refpective Rank of
each; and pleafed every one with his beft Abi-
lity, and at all Times was anxious for our Happinefs.—6thly, For erecting, at his own Ex-
pence, a Nabut Khana (a Place for a Kind of
Drum) at the Door of the Temple of Bifhefhur,
which is the Place of Worfhip of all Hindoftan.
—7thly, That at no Time did he omit any Particular tending to the Protection of the Inhabitants of this City; with refpect to us, that he
never was interefted, nor ever was defirous of
Detriment or Injury towards us.—We have reprefented, with Sincerity and Truth, what pleafing and proper Conduct Mr. Haftings obferved
towards us. The Fame of the King and Company is fpread through Indoftan; and we, who
have experienced Comfort and Eafe, offer up
our

our Prayers for the Profperity of his Majefty, and the Succefs of the Company.

" Written in the Month of Cartic Suddee 6th, 1844, Friday, by the Inhabitants of Benaris (Caafhy), October 1787.

Total Seals to this Addrefs, - 172

C.

Tranflation of the Paper marked C.

The Perfian Tranflation of a Paper written by the Bengal Pundits, in the Shawfcrit Language, under their Signatures.———" Reprefentation from the Inhabitants of the City of Benares, and Pilgrims of the Country, to the King of England and the Company.—We are fatisfied with the Conduct and Friendfhip of Mr. Haftings: During his Refidence in this Country, he always interefted himfelf in our Welfare, and in the Protection of our Reputation and Credit. As from the Effects of Mr. Haftings's Kindnefs, we refide in the City of Benaris with Comfort and Eafe, and the Promoters of Difturbances are feverely punifhed; many People come from all Quarters to refide here in confequence of knowing of this Happinefs. He has appointed the Nawaub Ally Ibrahim Cawn, from a Conviction of his Underftanding, Prudence, Fear of God, and Difinterestednefs, to protect the good and to punifh the bad Men; and to adjuft the Caufes between Mahomedans, according to the Koran; and between Hindoos, according to the Shaftar: And

And Ally Ibrahim Cawn poffeffed thofe Virtues,
and acts conformable to their Precepts; and in
confequence thereof, our Protection and Safety
is greater than during the Government of former Rajahs. When Mr. Haftings came to Benaris, every Perfon who went to fee him were
received with Attention and Refpect, according
to their Rank. And in order to pleafe God
(Bifhwifher), and to fecure eternal Protection,
he eftablifhed the Nubut, at his own great Ex-
pence, on the Door of the Temple of Bifhwifher.
During the Time of his Refidence in thefe Provinces, he cherifhed us as his Children. He did
not in the leaft Inftance occafion any Injury
towards us. On thefe Accounts we have always
lived in Peace; and the King of England, who
is our Protector and the Guardian of the Poor,
and the Company, have gained great Fame, and
we pray for their Profperity. This is the Reprefentation of the Inhabitants of Benaris."

Total Signatures to this Addrefs, - 113

d.

Tranflation of the Paper marked D.

*The Perfian Tranflation of a Paper, written by the
Noputty Bankers, Merchants, and others, under
their Signatures, in the Hindoo Language, and
Guzzeratty Characters.*

We are Merchants, Bankers, and Refidents
in Benaris; and reprefent, with Faith and
Truth, that Mr. Haftings never plundered any
Man's Property, never injured any one's Cha-

D racter

racter or Reputation, never received any Bribe, never poffeffed any Man's Territory or Property by Deceit, nor ever ruined the Country; but, on the contrary, laboured at the Profperity and Satisfaction of all Mankind, pleafed every one by his Kindnefs and Affability, appointed a Man of refpectable Character for the Protection of the City, and to adminifter Juftice in it, gave his Affiftance for the Promulgation of the Tenets of the Mahomedan and Hindoo Religions, and held a Conduct pleafing and fatisfactory.— As Mr. Haftings was poffeffed of Abilities, and acquainted with the Cuftoms of Hindoftan to a great Degree, he pleafed every Sect with his fuperior Manners; he was in the higheft Senfe defirous of Juftice, and Protection of the Ryotts; we were very much pleafed and happy at his Conduct.—We have reprefented what we knew.

The Signatures of the Noputty Bankers
and Merchants, &c.   -   -   405

E.

Copy Letter from the Refident at the Durbar; and of Tranflation of Perfian Papers which accompanied it.

To Edward Hay, Efquire, Secretary to the Government.

Sir,

HIS Highnefs the Nabob Mobarek ul Dowla has fent me the accompanying Papers, relating, as he informs me, to Mr. Haftings, de-
6   firing

firing I will immediately forward them to the
Right Honourable the Governor General.

I have numbered them 1 and 2 ; and am,

Sir,

Your moſt obedient,

humble Servant.

(Signed) PETER SPEKE,

Moradbaug,   Reſident Durbar.
14th Feb. 1788.

(A true Copy.)

E. Hay,

Secʸ to the Govᵗ.

*Papers received 16th February 1788, and tranſ-
lated, purſuant to an Order from the Governor
General in Council, dated 27th April 1788,
marked* F.

It is written for the Information and Knowledge of the Gentlemen in Power under the
King and Company of England, that we have
at this Time learnt by the News from Europe,
that a few Perſons, not being fully acquainted
with the real State and Cuſtoms of this Country, have repreſented Matters with reſpect to
Mr. Haſtings contrary to Truth and Fact, have
thrown the Minds of the Miniſters and People
of England into a State of Doubt, and have
injured Mr. Haſtings, and aſperſed his Character. As Mr. Haſtings, from the Time of
his Arrival until his Departure, adminiſtered
the Affairs of this Country with great Propriety
and Splendour; always ſought the Proſperity
and Welfare of the Family of Nawaub Meer
Mahomed Jaffier Khan, deceaſed, according to

D 2   the

the Purport of the Treaties and Engagements; laboured for the Satisfaction, for the Preservation of the Character and Honour of every one, according to his Rank and Station; and avoided every Circumstance which could occasion us Distress or Indignity; we were and are pleased and satisfied with him. It is therefore incumbent on us to write, without Diminution, and according to the Truth, what we have seen and heard of the Particulars of Mr. Haftings's Conduct.

1ft. The whole Period of Mr. Haftings's Refidence in this Country exhibited his good Conduct towards the Inhabitants. No Oppreffions nor Tyranny was admitted over any one. He obferved the Rules of Refpect and Attention to ancient Families. He did not omit the Performance of the Duties of Politenefs and Civility towards all Men of Rank and Station, when an Interview took place with them.

2dly. In Affairs concerning the Government and Revenues, he was not covetous of other Men's Money and Property; he was not open to Bribery. He reftricted the Farmers and Officers in their Oppreffions, in a Manner that prevented them from exercifing that Tyranny which Motives of Self-intereft and private Gain might inftigate them to obferve towards the Ryotts and Helplefs.

3dly. During his Adminiftration, no War or Commotion arofe in this Country; no Man's Property was plundered, but every one of every Rank lived in perfect Eafe and Security.

4thly. When, from the great Want of Rain, there were Appearances of a Famine, and it was

on

on the Eve of happening, when Thoufands would have perifhed, he laboured with every Exertion to prevent it; he brought Grain from the Inland Diftricts, and, in order to relieve the People, he abolifhed the Duties on Grain. He feverely threatened the Dealers in Grain, that no Hardfhip might be felt by any one.

5thly. He eftablifhed the Civil and Criminal (Dewanny and Fouzedarry) Courts upon proper Rules, fo that the Lives and Properties of Men were protected from the evil Acts of Thieves and Murderers. He regulated Punifhments according to the Rules of Koran, and ordained that each Sect fhould be tried according to its refpective Laws laid down in the Shafter and Koran.

6thly. He ufed great Exertions to cultivate the Country, to increafe the Agriculture and Revenues. He tranfacted the Bufinefs of the Country and Revenues without Deceit, and with perfect Propriety and Rectitude.

7thly. He refpected the learned and wife Men; and in order for the Propagation of Learning, he built a College, and endowed it with a Provifion for the Maintenance of the Students, infomuch that Thoufands, reaping the Benefits thereof, offer up their Prayers for the Profperity of the King of England, and for the Succefs of the Company.

8thly. He was not haughty in Temper, nor was he fond of State and Luxury; he did not feek his own Eafe, but at all Times laboured for the Profperity of the Country, and the Security of its Inhabitants.

9thly. So great was the Strength, and Power, and Grandeur, and Fame, and Magna-nimity,

nimity, of the Government of his Majefty, of
the Company, and the Englifh Nation, throughout all Hindoftan, during his Adminiftration,
that no one could eftablifh the Standard of Re-
bellion. In fhort, he was incomparable for his
Difpofition and Virtues; and, from the Length
of his Refidence in this Country, he was fully
acquainted with the Manners and Cuftoms of it,
and tranfacted all Affairs accordingly, and with
Credit and Propriety.

Dated 29th Zeffer 1202,
or 10th December 1787.

The Seals upon this Addrefs.

Nawaub Motimin Moulk Mobrack ul Dowla
Sied Mobrack Ally Khan Behadre Ferouze
Jung, Nazim of Soubahs Behar and Orifa.

Nawaub Munny, Beegum of Nawaub Meer Mahommed Jaffier Khan, deceafed, and Mother of Nawaub Nuzm ul Dowla, deceafed.

Jurmab Bubboo Beegum Soheba, Widow of
Nawaub Meer Mahomed Jaffier, deceafed,
Mother of Nawaub Motimin ul Moulk Be-
hadre Ferouze Jung.

Kyrum Neffa Beegum, Sifter of Nawaub Meer
Mahomed Jaffier Khan, deceafed.

Nuffiffaun Neffa Beegum, Sifter of Nawaub
Meer Mahomed Jaffier Khan, deceafed.

Nawaub Meer Murtiza Khan Bahadre Afud
Jung, Son of Sadue Ally Khan, deceafed, and
Grandfon of Nawaub Meer Mahomed Jaffier
Khan, deceafed.

Fetteh Ally Khan, Son of Nawaub Sadue Ally
Khan, deceafed, and Grandfon of Nawaub
Meer Mahomed Jaffier Khan, deceafed.

Sultaun

Sultàun Mirza Daoud, Son of Shah Selaman,
late King of Iran, and Son-in-Law to Nawaub
Sadue Ally Khan, deceafed.

Nawaub Iftakhar ul Moulk Affadud Dowla
Sied Khulleel ulla Khan Behadre Ghuzenfer
Jung, Son of Sultaun Mirzah Daowd, and
Son-in-Law to Nawaub Motimin ul Moulk
Behadre Feroze Jung.

Nawaub Imtiazul Dowla Sied Ahmeed Ally
Khan Behadre Gallib Jung, Son of Nawaub
Ihtaramul Dowla Behadre, who is Brother of
Nawaub Meer Mahomed Jaffier Khan, de-
ceafed.

Sied Baker Ally Khan, Hufband of the Sifter of
Nawaub Meer Mahomed Jaffier Khan, deceafed.

Juggut Seet Hurk Chund.

Seet Oby Chund, Uncle to Juggut Seet Hurk
Chund.

Sied Mahomed Hoffier Khan, eldeft Brother of
Nawaub Khan Khanna Behadre Mozuffer
Jung.

(A true Tranflation.)

(Signed)   G. F. CHERRY,
Depy Perf. Transr.

(A true Copy.)
E. Hay,
Secy to the Govt.

A fimilar Addrefs from the Inhabitants of
Rajemahl, figned by the Nabob Imtiaz ul
Dowlah, and 24 of the principal Inhabitants of
Rajemahl.

(32)

Under the Seals, as under written, marked H.

The humble Representations of us, Inhabitants and Residents of the Town of Moorsheda-bad, in the Kingdom of Bengal, to His Majesty, the Ministers, and the Directors of the East India Company of England, is as follows:

The late Governor, Warren Hastings, Esquire, during his Administration in this Country, from the Time of his Arrival until the Period of his Departure, at all Times gave us the greatest Satisfaction; and we were thankful for his good Conduct, and great good Qualities. He was always engaged in whatever tended to the Ease of the Ryotts, to the Security, Prosperity, and Cultivation of the Country. By his firm and well-formed Regulations, and by his new System for the Civil and Criminal (Dewanny and Fouzdarry) Courts, every one was protected from the Injuries of Robbers and Murderers; Justice was administered according to the Tenets of each respective Religion and Custom; and such was the due Vigilance and Care with which he protected this Country, that not one of the troublesome and rebellious Persons on its Borders could extend over it the Hand of Rapine and Invasion;—by these Means we lived in perfect Peace and Quiet. Notwithstanding a Scarcity of Rain, his Measures prevented the dreadful Effects of Famine. Mr. Hastings never shewed a Disposition coveting the Property or Riches, nor censuring or injuring the Reputation or Character of any one; nor did he ever accept of Bribes; but at all Times with courteous Manners, and proper Behaviour, per-

formed

formed the Civilities and Attentions due to Men
of Rank and Power, to Men of Learning and
Abilities. He eſtabliſhed Colleges for the Propagation of Learning, and endowed them with
Emoluments of a ſuitable Nature, inſomuch
that to this Time Thouſands profit by them,
and are employed in Prayers for the Proſperity
of His Majeſty, and for the Duration of the
Company's Adminiſtration. The Vigour and
Power of His Majeſty's Kingdom, the Strength
of the Company and Engliſh Nation, were ſo
evinced throughout Hindoſtan during the Government of Mr. Haſtings, that no one elevated
the Standard of Diſobedience. In ſhort, during
Mr. Haſtings's Government, we lived in perfect Peace and Security; we did not in the leaſt
Reſpect experience Diſtreſs or Uneaſineſs, but
are pleaſed and ſatisfied with his Virtues and
good Qualities.

The Seals upon this Addreſs.

Seals of Cauzies and Learned Men, and Men
of Character 24.

Seals of the Perſons of Family and Rank.

Omdutun Neſſa Boho Beegum, Widow of Na-
waub Seraje Ul Dowla, deceaſed,
Perf Ul Dien Ally Khan, Son of Aſruf Ally
Khan, 'Grandſon to Nawaub Jaffier Ally
Khan, deceaſed,
Sied Haady Ally Khan, Nephew to Nawaub
Jaffier Ally Khan, deceaſed,
Iziz Ally Khan, Son of Nawaub Shucker Ulla
Khan, and Grandſon to Nawaub Serfraje
Khan, deceaſed;

E   Hoſſein

Hoffein Raza Khan, Grandfon to Nawaub Mo-
habeft Jung, deceafed,

Sied Khadim Ally Khan, Son of Nawaub Kha-
din Hoffein Khan Behadre, deceafed,

Mahobut Ally Khan, Brother to Nawaub Seraje
Ul Dowla, deceafed,

Sied Ally Khan, High Steward the Nizamut,
Son of Sied Baker Ally Khan, Brother-in-
Law to Nawaub Jaffier Khan, deceafed,

Itbar Ally Khan Behadre, Superintendant to the
Houfehold of Nawaub Munny Beegum,

Hazy Saadut Mund Khan, Nezir to the Dewanny of Bubboo Beegum,

Hakim Sied Ally Khan, Son of Hackim Meer
Mahtaub, King's Officer,

Mahomed Afkerry, Son of Nawaub Futtah Ulla
Khan Behadre, deceafed,

Sied Hoffein Khan, Grandfon to Nawaub Ser-
fraz Khan, deceafed,

Aferd Ally Khan, Brother-in-Law to Mirza
Mahomed Eretch Khan, deceafed,

Murza Armed, Nephew to Nawaub Shahamuft
Jung, deceafed,

Oahed Ally Khan, Brother to Ally Ibrahim Khan
Behadre,

Omzud Ally Khan, Motahil to Nawaub Fouze
Jung Behadre,

Mirza Akber Ally, Nephew to Mirza Mahomed
Eutch Khan, Father-in Law to Nawaub Seraje Ul Dowla, deceafed,

Ahmed Hoffein Khan, Son of Abo Mahomed
Khan, and Grandfon to Mahomed Eutch
Khan, deceafed,

Sied Abid, Darogah of the Tofhakman of Nawaub Sezore Jung Behadre, and Nephew to
Jaffier Ally Khan, deceafed,

Merza

Merza Serjaat Ally, Nephew to Mirza Mahomed Eutch Khan, deceafed,

Sheek Golaum Roffool Khan Behadre, who was Commander of Cavalry in the Time of Nawaub Jaffier Ally Khan,

Neamut Ulla Khan, High Steward, Nawaub Khan Khanna Behadre Mozuffer Jung Mahomed Reza Khan,

Reza Ally Khan Arze Beggy Nawaub Motimen Ul Moulk Behadre Seroze Jung,

Sheer Ally Khan, an old Servant of Nawaub Meer Mahomed Jaffier Khan, and Son to Miza Hockin Beg, and Mofhab to Nawaub Mahabut Jung, deceafed,

Meer Mafir Ally, Nephew to Nawaub Jaffier Ally Khan, deceafed,

Nuzzie Ally Khan, Arge Beggy of Nawaub Ally Jah, and Son of Golaum Hoffein Khan,

Futteh Ally Khan, Relation of Mirza Mahomed Eritch Khan, deceafed,

Hoffein Ally Khan, Relation to Ditto,

Awuzy Ally Khan, Nephew to Nuferutta Khan,

Sied Fetrut Khan, Relation to Nawaub Gyrut Khan, deceafed,

Sied Ally Nucky, Mofhab to Nawaub Feroze Jung Behadre,

Mobareh Kooly Khan, Superintendant of Buildings to Nawaub Feroze Jung Behadre Mobarek ul Dowla,

Mirza Mahomed Ally Mofheb, Nawaub Ferze Jung Behadre,

Mirza Jumma Beg, Ditto, Ditto,

Haazy Roffum Ally, Darogah of the Privy Purfe, and Jebkhaus of Nawaub Ferize Jung Behadre,

Sied

Sied Lootf Ally, Relation to Nawaub Meer
Mahomed Jaffier Khan, deceafed,

Mirza Meer, an old Servant of Nawaub Meer
Mahomed Jaffier Khan, deceafed,

Mahomed Goozur Khan, an old Jemautdar of
Nawab Meer Mahomed Jaffier Khan, deceafed,

Sied Year Ally Khan,

Meer Juan Ulla, Naib to the High Steward of
the Nazamut,

Imam Bukfh Khan, Darogah of the Nezamut
Elephants,

Sied Mahomed Morad, Naib of Om-dut-un-
Neffa, Bhow Beegum,

Mirza Gudzuffer Ally,

Secundar Khan,

Buffunt Ally Khan,

Fyze Ullah Khan,

Azum Khan,

Ferhut Ulla Khan,

Mahomed Ryam Khan,

Jnad Ul Khan,

Affrut Ally Khan, Nazir of Omdut-un Neffa,
Bhow Beegum,

Golaum Hoffien Khan,

Mirza Mahomed Mohtuddy,

Sied Rootul Ally Saadaat Serfy,

Sied Mazum Ally,

Sied Kullub Ally,

Bahar Ally Khan,

Amanut Khan,

Nuzzer Ally Khan,

Sied Hoffien Khan Hoffeiny,

Mirza Mahomedy Khan,

Sied Zien ul Abdeen, of the Chiefs of Mecca,

Mohomed Baker, Son of Mohomed Hoffien,

Steward

Steward to Nazir ul Moufk, Son to Mobarek ul Dowla,

Mirza Azum Ally, Grandfon to Golawm Hoffien Khan Aoze Beggy,

Behadre Ally Khan.

Mahomedans 81.

Seals of Perfons in Office 42.

Seals of Bankers, &c. whofe Houfes are eftablifhed in feveral Places 10.

Copy Tranflation of Letter from the Nabob Vizier of Oude to the Governor General; and of Tranflation of Four Perfian Papers which accompanied it.

I.

From the Vizier, marked I.

Received 8th March 1788.

I HAVE learnt that Mr. Haftings has written to the Gentlemen refiding in Calcutta, to write the Particulars of the Conduct he obferved during his Government in India on the Part of the Company towards the Chiefs of Hindoftan, and that they fhould firft acquaint you therewith, and obtain your Confent. Your Lordfhip has been pleafed not to forbid thofe who were inclined to write with their own Free-will. The Chiefs and People of Bengal and Benaris have written Papers voluntarily; and as I am myfelf, and my Minifters and chief People about

me

me are, perfectly pleafed with Mr. Haftings's
Conduct, we have therefore written a Paper declaring our Satisfaction at it, and tranfmit it to
your Lordfhip. If your Lordfhip fhould be
pleafed, and the Papers written by the People of
Bengal, &c. fhould arrive with your Lordfhip,
and your Lordfhip fhould tranfmit them to Europe, you will alfo tranfmit thefe Papers with
them.

(A true Tranflate.)
(Signed) G. F. CHERRY,
D. P. T.

(A true Copy.)
E. Hay,
Sec^y to the Fort.

K.

*Papers received the 8th March 1788, and tranf-
lated purfuant to an Order from the Governor
General in Council, dated 27th April 1788.*

Under the Seal of his Excellency the Nawaub
Afoph Ul Dowla Afoph Jeh Behadar, Vizier Ul Momalik, marked K.

I have at this Time learnt that the Gentlemen in Power in England, upon the Sufpicion
that Mr. Haftings, during his Adminiftration,
acted contrary to the Rules of Juftice and Impartiality, and, actuated by Motives of Avidity,
was inimical towards Men without Caufe, that
he broke fuch Engagements and Treaties as had
been made between the Company and other
Chiefs, that he extended the Hand of Oppreffion
over the Properties of Men, tore up the Roots
of

of Security and Prosperity from the Land, and rendered the Ryotts and Subjects destitute by Force and Extortion *: As this Accusation in fact is destitute of Uprightness and void of Truth, therefore, with a View to shew the Truth in its true Colours, I have written upon this Sheet, with Truth and Sincerity, to serve as an Evidence, and to represent real Facts, to serve also as Information and Communication, that Mr. Hastings, from the Commencement of his Administration until his Departure for England, whether during the Lifetime of the deceased Nawaub, of blessed Memory, Vizier ul Moulk Sujah ul Dowlah Behadre, my Father, or during my Government, did not at any Time transact contrary to Justice any Matter which took place from the great Friendship between me and the Company, nor in any Business depart from the Path of Truth and Uprightness; but cultivated Friendship with Integrity and Sincerity, and in every Respect engaged himself in the Duties of Friendship with me, my Ministers and Confidents. I am at all Times and in every Way pleased with, and thankful for, his friendly Manners and Qualities; and my Ministers and Confidents, who have always, every one of them, been satisfied with his Conduct, are for ever grateful for his Friendship, and thankful for his Virtues. As

* Some Words are wanted in the Original to close and complete the Sense of this Passage. From the Context of this Address, and from the Words actually used in another Address which accompanies it, the Translator has no Doubt that the Words intended to be inserted are of this Import; viz. " are displeased with him."

these

thefe Matters are real Facts, and according to Truth, I have written thefe Lines as an Evidence, and tranfmit this Paper to England through the Government of Calcutta, for the Information of the Gentlemen of Power and Rank in England.

  (A true Tranflate.)

    (Signed) G. F. CHERRY,

       Dep. Per. Tranf.

(A true Copy.)

  E. Hay,

Secʳ to the Fort.

L.

Under the Seal of Nawaub Serfray ul Döwlah Nazim ul Mulk Hoffein Reza Khan Behadre, Zuffer Jung, and Nawaub Ameer ul Dowla Intezam ul Moulk Hyder Beg Khan Behaudre Nuzrut Jung, marked L.

It is at this Time learnt by the Nawaub Vizier, and us his Minifters, that the Gentlemen of Power in England are difpleafed with Mr. Haftings, on the Sufpicion that, during his Adminiftration in this Country, from Motives of Avidity, he committed Oppreffions contrary to the Rules of Juftice, took the Properties of Men by Deceit and Force, injured the Ryotts and Subjects, and rendered the Country deftitute and ruined. As the true and upright Difpofition of Mr. Haftings is in every Refpect free of this Sufpicion, we therefore, with Truth and Sincerity, declare by thefe Lines, written according to Fact, that Mr. Haftings, from the

10   Firft

First of his Appointment to the Government of
this Country until his Departure for Europe, during his Authority in the Management of the Affairs of the Country, whether in the Life-time of
the Nawaub Sujah ul Dowla Behadre, deceased,
or whether during the present Reign, did not, in
any Matters which took place from the great
Friendship between this Government and the
Company, act in anywise upon Motives of Avidity, and not having in any Respect other than
Justice and Propriety in Intention, did not
swerve from their Rules. He kept his Excellency the Vizier always pleased and satisfied
by his Friendship and Attention in every Matter. He at all Times shewed Favour and Kindness towards us the Ministers of this Government; and under his Protection having enjoyed
perfect Happiness and Comfort, we are from
our Hearts satisfied with and grateful for his
Benevolence and Goodness.—As by all the
Rules of Religion and Custom, to witness with
Truth procures its Reward of a good Name in
this World and hereafter, we have written
these Lines to prove our Satisfaction, and Mr.
Hastings's good Conduct, and transmit this
Paper to the Gentlemen in Europe.

A true Translate.

(Signed)   G. F. CHERRY.

D. P. Trans'.

A true Copy.

E. Hay,

Sec' to the Fort.

F   Under

Under the Seals as under-written, marked M.

At this Time it is heard that the Gentlemen in Power in Europe are displeased with Mr. Haftings, in consequence of Sufpicion thrown out by his Enemies, and reprefented to them, that Mr. Haftings, from Motives of Avidity, committed Acts during his Adminiftration and Authority contrary to the Rules of Juftice, and extended the Hand of Oppreffion and Ufurpation over the Property, Country, and Character of the Chiefs of thofe Countries who had Connection, or were in Friendfhip with the Company;——Therefore we, the People of Rank belonging to his Excellency the Vizier, upon the Principle that making a true and faithful Evidence is pleafing to the Almighty, declare what we have ourfelves feen during the Adminiftration of Mr. Haftings, and write as true, and faithfully witneffed with our Seals upon this Paper, that from the Commencement of Mr. Haftings's Government, we have not feen or experienced any Oppreffion or Tyranny in regard to our Defires, our Effects, or our Property; that we have paffed our Days in Peace and Security under his Protection; that no Injury or Detriment has ever happened from him to the Cultivation of the Lands; that no Oppofition or Hindrance has ever taken place from him in the Cuftoms of the Religion of any Sect; every Sect, whether Hindoo or Mahomedan, performing its religious Tenets according to its Profeffions and Rites in perfect Security; the Dignity and Character of every Perfon was fupported by him according to the refpective

Station

Station of each ; and every Perfon, pleafed and fatisfied with his good Conduct and Difpofition, were always, and continue to be, thankful ; Mankind, from the Efforts of his Mind, and the Power of his Meafures, were protected from Difturbances, and guarded againft Evils, paff- ing their Days in perfect Peace and Quiet. As thefe Particulars are individually true, we have therefore warranted this Paper with our Seals as an Evidence, and tranfmit it to the Gentlemen in England, in order that in giving Evidence of what is true and faithful no Neglect may be attributed to us, who have feen and witneffed the Manner and Conduct of Mr. Haftings dur- ing his Adminiftration.

The Names on the Seals affixed to this Addrefs,

The Seals.

Caffimally Khan Behadre Kyam Jung,
Akbar Ally Khan Behaudre Iftehar Jung,
Mirza Ifhmael Ally Khan Behadre,
Ally Kooly Khan Behaudre Sooraut Jung,
Ahmed Ally Khan Behaudre Shoukul Jung,
Vakeel Sultanut Moktaur Moulk Muder ul
    Dowla Behaudre,
Mahomed Ammee Khan Behaudre Buffalut
    Jung,
Newafifh Ally Khan Behaudre Sirdar Jung,
Ilmafs Ally Khan, Zekaak paij Mahomed,
Mufkerit Ul Ilmafs,
Rajah Jagenaut Behaudre,
Rajah Tuket Roy,
Ibrahim Ally Khan Behaudre,
Lutf Ally Khan,

Sheriff

Sheriff Ally Khan Behadre,
Ameer Khan Behadre,
Ramjee Sorhai Cashmeery Mull,
Rajah Butchraje.

N. B. On the Original is the Seal, **Yah Alla**
Moujood Ally Ullah Wullee.—This Seal is not
on the Copy.

A true Translate.
(Signed)   G. F. CHERRY,
Dep. Pers* Trans'.

A true Copy.
E. Hay,
S^y to the Gov^t.

Copy Translation of Letter from the Nabob of Furruckabad to the Governor General, and of Translate of Three Persian
Papers which accompanied it.

From the Nawaub of Furruckabad, marked N :
Received 31st *May* 1788.

I Have been informed that People in England
have accused Mr. Hastings of a Conduct that
carried with it the Destruction of the Country,
and that tended to disgrace the Inhabitants; and
that in order to do away this Accusation, the
Inhabitants of Bengal, Benares, and Lucknow,
have written, and continue to write, Address.
As I have been for a long Time connected with
the Company, and have not witnessed any Act
of Mr. Hastings, but that of Civility and Kindness, therefore having, from Principles of Gratitude, prepared an Address expressive of my
Satisfaction,

Satisfaction, I send it to your Lordship, and hope that you will transmit it to England, and thus make me indebted to your Kindness. Considering me attached to your Lordship, I trust you will make me happy by frequent Letters of Kindness.

A true Translate.

(Signed)   G. F. CHERRY,

D. P. T'.

A true Copy.

(Signed)   E. Hay,

Secr^y to the Fort.

Papers received 31st May 1788, and translated pursuant to an Order from the Governor General in Council, dated 27th April 1788.

Under the Seal of Nawaub Guzuffer ul Dowla Ameer ul Moulk Dileer Kimmut Furzend Khan Behader Mozuffer Jung, and the Seal of Ameer ul Dowla Mozuffer ul Moulk Mund Khan Behdre Bubber Jung, marked O.

Whereas Rectitude giveth Satisfaction unto God, the Communication of Truth is the Mean of Salvation, and the Cause of diffusing the Virtues of good Conduct. And as this is agreeable to every Understanding of Mankind in general, therefore is this Paper written freely, and according to the Inclination of my Heart, and whatever is just and true is represented with great Uprightness and Sincerity, [for the Information of His Majesty the King of England, the Ministers of the Nation, and the Company —That Mr. Hastings, from the Commencement

ment of his Adminiftration of the Affairs of Hindoftan, never committed any Act of Oppreffion towards me, Deleer Himmat Khan Mozuffer Jung; on the contrary, I lived under his Kindnefs and Protection in perfect Eafe and Safety, and guarded againft my Enemies by his Conduct. I entertained Hopes from him that he would have reprefented the true State of my Government to His Majefty and the Company, and have fo exerted himfelf as to have procured it to be reftored to its former State. As I have now heard that Mr. Haftings's Enemies, uniting together, have accufed him before the Gentlemen of England of having taken the Property of Men in Hindoftan, of having deprived the Inhabitants of the Lands they had cultivated, and injured their Reputations by putting Difgrace upon them; it is incumbent on us Mahomedans, according to the Orders of God and his Prophet, and our religious Forefathers, to declare, having our religious Tenets in View, what we know to be juft and true: We now declare to all Men of all Ranks in England the Juftice and good Conduct, the Kindnefs and pleafing Manners of Mr. Haftings, which we have witneffed; and at a Time when we are thankful and grateful for his Behaviour we have affixed our Names to this Paper of Satiffaction, and tranfmit through the Government of Calcutta to England.

Dated 21ft Zeffer 1202, or in December 1787.

A true Tranflate.

(Signed) G. F. CHERRY, D. P. Trans".

A true Copy.
E. Hay,
Sec^y to the Fort.

Under

Under the Seals as under-written, marked P.

We the Cauzie, Mofti, Students, Men of Rank, Men of Bufineſs, Merchants, Bankers, and Tradeſmen, Inhabitants of the Town of Furruckabad, bear Evidence to the King of England, Miniſters, and Directors of the Company, That Mr. Haſtings committed no Kind of Oppreſſion on us from the Commencement of his Adminiſtration in Hindoſtan, until his Departure. But on the contrary, under his Kindneſs and Protection we lived in Peace and Security, and were guarded againſt our Enemies. As we have now heard that Mr. Haſtings's Enemies have laid an Accuſation againſt him before the Miniſters of England, that he took the Property of People in Hindoſtan, laid waſte their Lands, and blaſted their Reputation by Diſgraces, it is neceſſary that we Mahomedans, agreeable to the Orders of God and his Prophets, and that we Hindoos, according to the Beeds and the Shaſter, repreſent and make known what is Fact: We therefore repreſent to all Mankind the Juſtice and Kindneſs of Mr. Haſtings, which we have always ſeen; and now, when we are grateful and thankful for his Kindneſs, we write this Deed of Satisfaction, and from our own free Will affix our Seals thereto, and tranſmit it through our own Sovereign and Chief to Calcutta, in order that the Government there may ſend it to England.

Dated 21 Zeffer, 1202, Hijeree,
  or December 1787.

Seals and Signatures to this Addreſs   53.

Copy Letter from the Collector of Dinagepore, dated 8th July; and Copy Tranflate of a Perfian Paper which accompanied it.

Edward Hay, Efquire, Secretary to the
Government.

Sir,

AT the Requeft of the Zemindary Officers of
Purgunna Havillee Penjeerah, &c. I
tranfmit the enclofed Perfian Paper, containing
Teftimonies relative to Mr. Haftings.

I am, Sir,
Your very obedient,
humble Servant,
Dinagepore,   (Signed) G. HATCH,
July 8th 1788.   Collector Dinagepore.

(A true Copy.)
E. Hay,
S.r to the Gov.t.

*Paper received 18th July 1788, tranfmitted by
George Hatch, Efquire, Collector of Dinagepore, and tranflated purfuant to an Order from
the Governor General in Council, dated 27th
April 1788, marked* Q.

I. Radanaut, Zemindar of Purgunnah Ha-
velly Penjuna, &c. commonly called Dinagepore: As it has been learnt by me, the Mutte-
fuddies, and refpectable Officers of my Zemindary,

13

dary, that the Minifters of England are difpleafed with the late Governor, Warren Haftings
Efquire, upon the Sufpicion that he oppreffed
us, took Money from us by Deceit and Force,
and ruined the Country ; therefore we, upon the
Strength of our Religion, which we think it incumbent on and neceffary for us to abide by,
following the Rules laid down in giving Evidence, declare the Particulars of the Acts and
Deeds of Warren Haftings Efquire, full of
Circumfpeetion and Caution, Civility and Juftice,
fuperior to the Conduct of the moft learned ;
and by reprefenting what is Fact, wipe away the
Doubts that have poffeffed the Minds of the
Minifters of England: That Mr. Haftings is
poffeffed of Fidelity and Confidence, and yielding Protection to us, that he is clear of the Contamination of Miftruft and Wrong, and his
Mind is free of Covetoufnefs or Avarice. During the Time of his Adminiftration no one faw
other Conduct than that of Protection to the
Hufbandmen, and Juftice ; no Inhabitant ever
experienced Afflictions, no one ever felt Oppreffion from him; our Reputations have always
been guarded from Attacks by his Prudence,
and our Families have always been protected by
his Juftice. He never omitted the fmalleft Inftance of Kindnefs towards us, but healed the
Wounds of Defpair with the Salve of Confolation, by means of his benevolent and kind Behaviour, never permitting one of us to fink in
the Pit of Defpondence ; he fupported every
one by his Goodnefs, overfet the Defigns of
evil-minded Men by his Authority, tied the
Hand of Oppreffion with the ftrong Bandage
of Juftice, and by thefe Means expanded the
pleafing

pleasing Appearance of Happiness and Joy over us: He re-established Justice and Impartiality. We were, during his Government, in the Enjoyment of perfect Happiness and Ease, and many of us are thankful and satisfied. As Mr. Hastings was well acquainted with our Manners and Customs, he was always desirous, in every Respect, of doing whatever would preserve our religious Rites, and guard them against every Kind of Accident and Injury, and at all Times protected us. Whatever we have experienced from him, and whatever happened from him, we have written without Deceit or Exaggeration.

Seals to this Address.

Maha Rajah Radanaus Behadre,
Ram Caunt Roy Naib, Zemindar,
Kisperam Sein Mhal, Zemindarry Aumeen,
Kishen Caunt Roy, Zemindarry Tehsildar,
Meel Caunt, Zemindarry Peishcar,
Rada Rohmun Sohay, Peishcar Aumeen,
Nundololl Sohay, Zemindarry Peishcar,
Raje Kishen Berjoo, Zemindarry Chuckladut.

A true Translate.
(Signed) G. F. CHERRY,
Dep. Pers² Translator.
A true Copy.
E. Hay,
Sec^y to the Gov^t.

Copy Tranflations of a Letter and Papers, tranfmitted to the Governor General by the Nabob of Dacca.

From the Nawaub of Dacca to Earl Cornwallis: Received 19th August 1788.

AT this Time People of all Ranks, Inhabitants of Dacca, have heard that fince Mr. Haftings's Arrival in England an Inveftigation into his Conduct while Governor is carrying on before the High Court of Juftice of England; therefore the Inhabitants of Dacca of Office and Credit have brought to me an Addrefs, authenticated by the Cauzy, and fealed with their refpective Seals, reprefenting their Satisfaction, and requefted me to affix my Seals thereto. I fent for them into the Hall of Audience, and learnt from each of them the Purport of the Addrefs; when having enquired into it, I put my own Seal to it; and have the Pleafure to enclofe in my prefent Letter to your Lordfhip the Addrefs, a Lift of the Names, and an Addrefs from myfelf, with Duplicates of each. Your Lordfhip will perufe them, and be kind enough to tranfmit them to England. I hope your Lordfhip will conceive me to be a fincere Well-wifher and Friend, and honour me frequently with Letters of Kindnefs.

A true Tranflate.

(Signed) G. F. CHERRY,
D. P. T^r.

A true Copy.
   E. Hay,
      Sec^y to the Gov^t.

G 2

S.

Papers received 19th *August* 1788, *and translated pursuant to an Order from the Governor General in Council, dated* 27th *April* 1788.

Translation of Addrefs marked N° 1. under the Seal of Nuzur ul Moulk Intizam ul Dowla Seyed Allykhan Behadre Nuzrut Jung, and that of his Brother Shumzul ul Dowla, Syed Akmud Allykhan.

From the Reports of all Ranks of People, and from the News-papers, the Inhabitants of Hindoftan, but particularly thofe of Bengal and its Dependencies, have learnt, that after the Arrival of Warren Haftings Efquire, in England, an Inveftigation into the Conduct he obferved in Hindoftan while Governor of Calcutta has been commenced before the High Court of Juftice of England; and that the Parliament, who are defirous of Juftice, and permit no improper Act to pafs, are determined to make a thorough Inveftigation into every Matter, and feparate Right from Wrong: In confequence, all Claffes of the Inhabitants of Hindoftan have unanimoufly agreed, that as they all live in Eafe and Peace under the kind Influence of the Protection of His Majefty the King of England, and the Parliament, and that on account of the Care taken of them by the Parliament, they are daily more and more attached and zealous; and as Mr. Haftings during the Period of his Adminiftration

miniftration always fhewed great Kindnefs and
Protection, and obferved ftrict Juftice towards
them, and in confequence of his good Qualities, his Care, and Juftice, has great Claim
upon them, and that it is incumbent on them
for ever to keep in Remembrance this Obliga-
tion :—Therefore it is neceffary for them to reprefent every Particular which they are acquainted with, of fuch Matters as the Juftice of the
Parliament is about to inquire into, in fuch
Manner as that their Reprefentations fhall be
noticed, and in a fhort Space of Time beftowed
thereto the Truth of every Matter be known.
Notwithftanding the Minds of juft Men are like
the Mirror, and what is right is immediately
difcovered, and Juftice is not thrown into Doubt
by the Declarations of any one, yet religious
Rites of every Sect, and the Books of every
Prophet, give Sanction to Evidence, and it
is a Demonftration in every Matter under Inveftigation; therefore, all the Inhabitants of
this Country are unanimous in the above-written
Intention: Among others, thofe of Jehanguir-
nar, commonly called Daccas, folely in order
to reprefent Facts, which by all Books of Religion and expounded Laws is incumbent on
every one, have brought to me an Addrefs,
fealed with their Seals, and teftified by the Cauzy,
that I may affix my own Seal thereto, and tranfmit it to the Court of Juftice; Wherefore, I
Syed Ally, commonly called Nuzrut Jung,
Grandfon of the deceafed Nawaub Jeffarut
Khan, now, by the Kindnefs, Document of
Right and Protection of old Servants, difplayed
by His Majefty, the Parliament, and Directors

of

of the Company of England, in Charge of the
Office of the Nizamut of the said City, called
all those who have affixed their Seals on the said
Address into the Hall of Audience, and have
learnt verbally from each the Purport of the
Writing, and having examined into it have
affixed my own Seal thereto; for the Concealment of Truth is a great Crime before God,
and revealing it is praise-worthy and pleasing to
Mankind; and as among them there are many
holy and religious Men, many learned, true, and
upright Men, and many Descendants from Families of high Fame and Rank, who have affixed
their Seals, I therefore perceived the Propriety
of vouching to their Declarations, that the Particulars may be known, and their Representations obtain Sanction in the Minds of their
Hearers. " God is the Discriminator of Truth,
" and an upright and just Judge, and I seek
" Protection under him against Falsity and Un-
" truth."

Written 15th Ramzaan 1202
  Hijeree, or 9th Assar 1195,
  B'. corresponding with the
  8th June 1788, E. S.

A true Translate.
  (Signed)   G. F. CHERRY,
            D. P. T'.

A true Copy.
  E. Hay,
    Secr' to the Gov',

T.

Translation of the Address under the Seals, as under written, marked N° 2.

The Natives and Refidents of the City of Jehanguirnagur humbly reprefent to His Moft Gracious Majefty the King of England, and to the Comptrollers and Directors of the Company, That the former Governor, Mr. Haftings, during the Period of his Adminiftration, by the Juftice he obferved, by his Complacency and good Qualities, and by his Protection, fecured our Satisfaction and Gratitude. He engaged himfelf in the Relief of our Situations, and in our Profperity. He protected us from Thieves and Affaffins by the Syftems he laid down for the Civil and Criminal (Dewanny and Fouzdary) Courts, which were purely upon Motives of Goodnefs to Mankind, actuated by a Love for Juftice; he permitted the Exercife of the Religion of each Sect according to the refpective Tenets and Cuftoms. He never neglected the Safety and Peace of the Inhabitants, nor the Cultivation of the Country. During his Government we flept in the Cradle of Security. He never coveted our Money or Property, nor attacked our Reputation, nor had he ever Inclination to do wrong, but treated every one according to the refpective Station of each. He obferved a Conduct of Refpect and Veneration towards the learned and experienced Men, and towards Men of Family, according to the Degree

gree of their Abilities and Science, of whatever
Sect and Religion; and during his Administration he treated all the Inhabitants with Kindness
and Encouragement; and from his good Qualities, his Justice, and his Attention, he has a
great Claim upon us. In such Matters as would
secure the Prayers of us Wellwishers for the
everlasting Duration of His Majesty's Throne,
and of the Jurisdiction and Government of the
Company, he was constantly engaged; for Instance, to this Day the Colleges which he built,
and where he established Allowances for the
Students, remain, and the Students receive the
fixed Allowance, and pass their Lives in Peace
and Thanksgiving; and it is incumbent on us
for ever to keep in recollection the Obligations
we are under to him. It is therefore necessary
that in Matters which have induced the Minds
of the Just to investigate, we obey the Orders of
God in declaring what we know; we have therefore done so. Further Orders will be issued by
his Majesty.——Dated the 15th Ramzaan 1202,
Hejerie, 9th Assar 1195 B'. according to the
20th June 1788 E'.

The Seals to this Address,   78.

Copy of Two Letters from the Collector of Dinagepore, and of Translation of Persian Papers, transmitted by him.

Edward Hay, Esquire, Secretary to the Government.

Sir,

AT the Request of Godadur Gose, the Vakeel of Seid Buddie ul Z'man, I forward the accompanying Persian Paper, containing Testimonies relative to Mr. Hastings.

I am, Sir,
Your most obedient
humble Servant,

Dinagepore,   (Signed) G. HATCH,
16th July 1788.   Coll^r Din^e.

A true Copy.
E. Hay,
Sec^y to the Gov^t.

U.

Paper received 23d August 1788, transmitted by the Collector of Silberres, and translated pursuant to an Order from the Governor General in Council, dated 27th July 1788.

Under the Seal and Signature of Buddie ul Zeman, Father of Golaum Suttaun, Zemindar of 8 Anna Division of Pergunnah Silberries.

As it has been learnt by me, the Muttesuddees, and respectable Officers of my Zemindary,

that the Minifters of England are difpleafed
with the late Governor Warren Haftings,
Efquire, upon the Sufpicion that he oppreffed
us, took Money from us by Deceit and Force,
and ruined the Country; therefore we, upon
the Strength of our Religion, which we think
it incumbent on and neceffary for us, to abide
by, the following Rules laid down in giving
Evidence, declare the Particulars of the Acts
and Deeds of Warren Haftings, Efquire, full
of Circumfpection and Caution, Civility and
Juftice, fuperior to the Conduct of the moft
learned; and, by reprefenting what is Fact,
wipe away the Doubts that have poffeffed the
Minds of the Minifters of England; that Mr.
Haftings is poffeffed of Fidelity and Confidence,
and yielding Protection to us; that he is clear
of the Contamination of Miftruft and Wrong,
and his Mind is free from Covetoufnefs or Avarice. During the Time of his Adminiftration
no one faw other Conduct than that of Protection to the Hufbandmen, and Juftice; no Inhabitants ever experienced Affliction; no one ever
felt Oppreffion from him; our Reputations have
always been guarded from Attacks by his Prudence, and our Families have always been protected by his Juftice; he never omitted the
fmalleft Inftance of Kindnefs towards us, but
healed the Wounds of Defpair with the Salve
of Confolation, by means of his benevolent and
kind Behaviour, never permitting one of us to
fink in the Pit of Defpondency; he fupported
every one by his Goodnefs, overfet the Defigns
of evil-minded men by his Authority, tied the
Hand of Oppreffion with the ftrong Bandage of
Juftice, and by thefe Means expanded the

pleafing

pleafing Appearance of Happinefs and Joy over
us; he re-eftablifhed Juftice and Impartiality.
We were, during his Government, in the Enjoyment of perfect Happinefs and Eafe, and
many, many of us are thankful and fatisfied.
As Mr. Haftings was well acquainted with our
Manners and Cuftoms, he was always defirous,
in every Refpect, of doing whatever would preferve our religious Rites, and guard them'
againft every Kind of Accident and Injury, and
at all Times protected us.——Whatever we have
experienced from him, and whatever happened
from him, we have written without Deceit or
Exaggeration.

    A true Tranflate.
        (Signed) G. F. CHERRY,
               D. P. Tʳ.

A true Copy.
    E. Hay,
      Secʸ to the Govᵗ.

V.

Under the Seal of Atta Hoffeen, Son of Rezyul
Dein Choudry, of Purgunnah Selberries in
Bengal.

As it has been learnt by me, the Muttefud-
dies and refpectable Officers of my Zemindary,
that the Minifters of England are difpleafed with
the late Governor Warren Haftings, Efquire,
upon the Sufpicion that he oppreffed us, took
Money from us by Deceit and Force, and ruined the Country; therefore we, upon the Strength
of

of our Religion. which we think it incumbent on and neceſſary for us to abide by, the following Rules laid down in giving Evidence, declare the Particulars of the Acts and Deeds of Warren Haſtings, Eſquire, full of Circumſpection and Caution, Civility and Juſtice, ſuperior to the Conduct of the moſt learned; and by repreſenting what is Fact, wipe away the Doubts that have poſſeſſed the Minds of the Miniſters of England; that Mr. Haſtings is poſſeſſed of Fidelity and Confidence, and yielding Protection to us; that he is clear of the Contamination of Miſtruſt and Wrong, and his Mind is free from Covetouſneſs or Avarice. During the Time of his Adminiſtration no one ſaw other Conduct than that of Protection to the Huſbandmen, and Juſtice; no Inhabitant ever experienced Affliction; no one ever felt Oppreſſion from him. Our Reputations have always been guarded from Attacks by his Prudence, and our Families have always been protected by his Juſtice. He never omitted the ſmalleſt Inſtance of Kindneſs towards us, but healed the Wounds of Deſpair with the Salve of Conſolation, by means of his benevolent and kind Behaviour, never permitting one of us to ſink in the Pit of Deſpondence. He ſupported every one by his Goodneſs, overſet the Deſigns of evil-minded Men by his Authority, tied the Hands of Oppreſſion with the ſtrong Bandage of Juſtice, and by theſe Means expanded the pleaſing Appearance of Happineſs and Joy over us. He re-eſtabliſhed Juſtice and Impartiality. We were, during his Government, in the Enjoyment of perfect Happineſs and Eaſe, and many, many of us are thankful and ſatisfied.

As

As Mr. Haftings was well acquainted with our
Manners and Cuftoms, he was always defirous
in every Refpect of doing whatever would preferve our religious Rites, and guard them
againft every Kind of Accident and Injury, and
at all Times protected us.—Whatever we have
experienced from him, and whatever happened
from him, we have written without Deceit or
Exaggeration.

A true Tranflate.

(Signed)   G. F. CHERRY,

D. P. T^r,

A true Copy.

E. Hay,

Sec^{ry} to the Gov^t.

Edward Hay, Efquire, Secretary to the Government.

Sir,

At the Requeft of Roopoam, the Vakeel of
Rezzie-d-die, I tranfmit the enclofed Perfian
Paper, containing Teftimonies relative to Mr.
Haftings.

I am, Sir,

Your moft obedient,

humble Servant,

(Signed)   G. HATCH,

Coll^r Ding^e.

Dinagepore,
the 14th Auguft 1788.

A true Copy.

E. Hay,

Sec^y to the Gov^t.

Copy of Letter from the Collector of Nuddea, and of Translation of Persian Papers transmitted by him.

To Edward Hay, Esquire, Secretary to the Government, Fort William.

Sir,

IN consequence of your Letter of the 31st March, I have now the Pleasure of transmitting to you Three Addresses in favour of Mr. Hastings.—The First having been presented to me by the Rajah of this District; the Second by the Four Zemindars of Houghly, the Zemindar of Satsyka, and Sixty Talookdars, who pay their Revenues to me; and a Third in the Shanskrit Language, which I have received from the Rajah of this District, signed by Two hundred and Eighty-nine Bramins, Inhabitants of Nuddea, Santipore, and other Places, many of them being the principal Pundits in this Country. This Address had been prepared by the late Rajah Sheo Chund, who intended to have presented it to me himself before his Death.

I have the Honour to be,
Sir,
Your most obedient Servant,
(Signed) F. REDFEARN,
Coll'.

Kishinagur,
the 1st October 1788.

A true Copy.
E. Hay,
Sec'y to the Fort.

Papers tranfmitted by the Collector of Nuddea, received 4th October 1788, and tranflated purfuant to an Order from the Governor General in Council, under Date 27th April 1788.

W. Under the Seal of Maha Rajah Dheraje Scolhund Behadre.

The Refidents, whether Hindoo or Followers of Mahomed, in the Country, have heard that the Gentlemen in England are difpleafed with Mr. Haftings, on Sufpicion that he oppreffed us Inhabitants of this Place, took our Money by Deceit and Force, and ruined the Country.—Therefore we, upon the Strength of our Religion and religious Tenets, which we hold as a Duty upon us, and in order to act conformable to the Decrees of God, in delivering Evidence, relate the praife-worthy Actions, full of Prudence and Rectitude, Friendfhip and Politenefs, of Mr. Haftings, poffeffed of great Abilities and Underftanding; and by reprefenting Facts remove the Doubts that have poffeffed the Minds of the Gentlemen in England; that Mr. Haftings diftributed Protection and Security to Religion, and Kindnefs and Peace to us all. He is free from the Charge of Embezzlements and Fraud, and his Heart is void of Covetoufnefs and Avidity. During the Period of his Government no one experienced from him other than Protection and Juftice, never having felt Hardfhip from him; nor did the Poor even know the Weight of an oppreffive Hand from him. Our Characters and Reputations have been always guarded in Quiet from Attack by the Vi-

gilance

gilance of his Prudence and Foresight, and preserved by the Terror of his Justice. He never
omitted the smallest Instance of Kindness and
Goodness towards us, and those entitled to it,
but always applied, by Soothings and Mildness,
the Salve of Comfort to the Wounds of Affliction, not allowing a single Person to be overpowered by Despair. He displayed his Friendship and Kindness to all. He destroyed the
Powers of Enemies and wicked Men by the
Strength of his Terror. He tied the Hands of
Tyrants and Oppressors by his Justice ; and, by
this Conduct, he secured Happiness and Joy to
us. He re-established the Foundation of Justice;
and we, at all Times, during his Government,
lived in Comfort, and passed our Days in Peace.
We are many, many of us satisfied and pleased
with him. As Mr. Hastings was perfectly well
acquainted with the Manners and Customs of
these Countries, he was always desirous of performing that which would tend to the Preservation of our Religion, and of the Duties of our
Sects, and guard the religious Customs of each
from the Effects of Misfortunes and Accidents.
In every Sense he treated us with Attention and
Respect. I have represented, without Deceit,
what I have myself seen, and the Facts that happened from him.

A true Translate.
(Signed) G. F. CHERRY,
Dep^y Perⁿ Trans^r.

A true Copy.
   E. Hay,
      Sec^{ry} to the Fort.

The Translation of a Paper, written by the Pundits and Bramins of Nuddea Santipoor, &c. in the Shanscrit Language, under the Signatures as under-written.

X.

That peaceable Difposition, that mild Temper, poffeffing the firft Qualities and the greateft Kindnefs, adorned with Civility and fincere Affability to a Degree as to become the Theme among the Learned of every Clafs, and the Senfible in every Science, endowed with every praife-worthy Quality and Virtue, enlightening the World like the Moon, of Mr. Haftings, the Minifters of England are difpleafed with, on the Sufpicion that he ruined the Property of the Inhabitants of this Country, under the Company's Authority, taking their Wealth by Force and Deceit. We the Inhabitants of this Country, on hearing this, reprefent and relate the pleafing and kind Qualities and Virtues of Mr. Haftings, who fought the Right, and was Judge of it, in order to remove this Doubt from the Minds of the Chiefs in England, that Mr. Haftings behaved with Honour and Refpect to all the Refidents of this Country of all Ranks, according to their refpective Situations in Life, their Profeffions, their Religions, and Sects, and treated them with paternal Kindnefs, free from Deceit or Avarice, and fhewed Refpect and Attention to all learned Men and Students in any Science. He was a long Time refident

I   in

in this Country, and well acquainted with every proper Cuftom and Mode for adminiftering Juftice. During the Period of his Adminiftration, every one, whether great or fmall, living in perfect Happinefs, profeffed their own Religions, and exercifed their own worldly Concerns with perfect Eafe and Quiet. This is the inward Sentiment of all the Inhabitants of this Country.

The Signatures to this Addrefs, 288.

Under the Signatures and Seals as under written.

y. We the Zemindars, Chowderies, and Talookdars of Pergunnah Mahomed Amunpoor, and other Mhals, belonging to the Zillah of Nudea in Bengal, have heard that the Gentlemen in England are difpleafed with Mr. Haftings, on Sufpicion that he oppreffed us Inhabitants of this Place, took our Money by Deceit and Force, and ruined the Country; therefore we, upon the Strength of our Religion and religious Tenets, which we hold as a Duty upon us, and in order to act conformable to the Decrees of God in delivering Evidence, relate the praifeworthy Actions, full of Prudence and Rectitude, Friendfhip and Politenefs, of Mr. Haftings, poffeffed of great Abilities and Underftanding; and by reprefenting Facts remove the Doubts that have poffeffed the Minds of the Gentlemen in England; that Mr. Haftings diftributed Protection and Security of Religion, and Kindnefs and Peace to us all; he is free from the Charge of Embezzlements and Fraud, and his Heart is void of Covetoufnefs and Avidity. During

During the Period of his Government, no one experienced from him other than Protection and Juſtice, never having felt Hardſhip from him, nor did the Poor ever know the Weight of an oppreſſive Hand from him; our Characters and Reputations have been always guarded in Quiet from Attack, by the Vigilance of his Prudence and Foreſight, and preſerved by the Terror of his Juſtice; he never omitted the ſmalleſt Inſtance of Kindneſs and Goodneſs towards us, and thoſe entitled to it, but always applied, by Soothings and Mildneſs, the Salve of Comfort to the Wounds of Affliction, not allowing a ſingle Perſon to be overpowered by Deſpair; he diſplayed his Friendſhip and Kindneſs to all; he deſtroyed the Powers of Enemies and wicked Men by the Strength of his Terror; he tied the Hands of Tyrants and Oppreſſors by his Juſtice, and by this Conduct he ſecured Happineſs and Joy to us; he re-eſtabliſhed the Foundation of Juſtice, and we at all Times, during his Government, lived in Comfort, and paſſed our Days in Peace. We are many, many of us ſatisfied and pleaſed with him. As Mr. Haſtings was perfectly well acquainted with the Manners and Cuſtoms of theſe Countries, he was always deſirous of performing that which would tend to the Preſervation of our Religion, and of the Duties of our Sects, and guard the religious Cuſtoms of each from the Effects of Misfortunes and Accidents. In every Senſe he treated us with Attention and Reſpect.—We have repreſented without Deceit what we have ourſelves ſeen, and the Facts that happened from him.

The Signatures to this Addreſs, 68.

Copy Letter from the Collector of Boglepore; and Copy Tranflation of a Perfian
Paper tranfmitted therewith.

To Edward Hay, Efq. Secretary to the Government General at Fort William.

Sir,

YOUR Letter of the 31ft March, by the Di-
rection of the Right Honourable the Governor General in Council, authorifed me to receive and tranfmit to you any Addreffes from
the Native Inhabitants of this Diftrict, which
they might be defirous of prefenting, in Teftimony relative to Mr. Haftings.

I have herewith the Honour to tranfmit you
fundry Papers on this Subject, Nᵒ 1, 2, 3, and 4,
which have been tendered to me by and on the
Part of the Zemindars, Canongoes, and the other
principal Inhabitants of the Diftricts of Boglepore and Rajemahl, and of the Hill People,
Inhabitants of the Jungleterry Diftricts. The
Papers No. 1 and 2 appear to contain the Signatures of all the Landholders and Canongoes
of my Divifion; and I think it neceffary to acquaint you, that thefe, as well as the others,
were voluntarily tendered to me, without the
fmalleft Interference on my Part to obtain
them.

I have the Honour to be,

Sir,

Boglepore,   Your moft obedient,
23d Sept. 1788.   Humble Servant,
(Signed) ROBᵀ ADAIR.

A true Copy.   Collector.
    E. Hay,
      Secry. to the Fo'.

8

a a.   *Papers received the 2d October 1788,
transmitted by the Collector of Boglepore, and translated pursuant to an
Order from the Governor General in
Council, dated 27th April 1788, under
the Seals and Signatures as under
written.*

We Canongoes, Zemindars, Choudries, and
Talookdars of the Diſtrict of Boglepore, in the
Province of Behar, have heard that the Gentlemen in England are diſpleaſed with Mr. Haſtings,
on Suſpicion that he oppreſſed us Inhabitants
of this Place, took our Money by Deceit and
Force, and ruined the Country.—Therefore we,
upon the Strength of our Religion and religious Tenets, which we hold as a Duty upon
us, and in order to act conformable to the Decrees of God, in delivering Evidence, relate the
praiſe-worthy Actions full of Prudence and
Rectitude, Friendſhip and Politeneſs, of Mr.
Haſtings, poſſeſſed of great Abilities and Underſtanding; and by repreſenting Facts, remove
the Doubts that have poſſeſſed the Minds of the
Gentlemen in England: That Mr. Haſtings
diſtributed Protection and Security to Religion,
and Kindneſs and Peace to us all.   He is free
from the Charge of Embezzlement and Fraud,
and his Heart is void of Covetouſneſs and Avidity.   During the Period of his Government,
no one experienced from him other than Protection and Juſtice, never having felt Hardſhips
from him; nor did the Poor ever know the
Weight of an oppreſſive Hand from him.   Our
Characters and Reputations have been always
guarded

guarded in Quiet from Attack, from the Vigilance of his Prudence and Forefight, and preferved by the Terror of his Juftice. He never omitted the fmalleft Inftance of Kindnefs and Goodnefs towards us, and thofe entitled to it; but always applied, by Soothings and Mildnefs, the Salve of Comfort to the Wounds of Affliction, not allowing a fingle Perfon to be overpowered by Defpair. He difplayed his Friendfhip and Kindnefs to all; he deftroyed the Power of Enemies and wicked Men by the Strength of his Terror; he tied the Hands of Tyrants and Oppreffors by his Juftice; and by this Conduct he fecured Happinefs and Joy to us. He re-eftablifhed the Foundation of Juftice; and we at all Times, during his Government, lived in Comfort, and paffed our Day in Peace. We are many, many of us, fatisfied and pleafed with him. As Mr. Haftings was perfectly well acquainted with the Manners and Cuftoms of thefe Countries, he was always defirous of performing that which would tend to the Prefervation of our Religion, and of the Duties of our Sects, and guard the religious Cuftoms of each from the Effects of Misfortunes and Accidents. In every Senfe he treated us with Attention and Refpect.—We have reprefented without Deceit what we have ourfelves feen, and the Facts that happened from him.

The Seals and Signatures to this Addrefs, 43.

Under the Seals and Signatures as under written.

66. We humbly reprefent to the Minifter of the King of England, That we, Inhabitants of Zillah

Zillah Boglepoor, and Chuckla Akbarnagur, have heard that a few Perfons, totally ignorant of the Particulars relative to this Country, have made falfe calumnious Reports regarding Mr. Haftings, thereby throwing the Minds of the Minifters of England into Doubt, and injured Mr. Haftings, and afperfed his Character: This has much aftonifhed us, as all the Inhabitants of this Country lived in perfect Eafe and Quiet, by the good Conduct which he followed from the Time of his Arrival until his Departure. Mr. Haftings tranfacted the Affairs of the Country in a proper Manner, at all Times feeking the Profperity and Happinefs of the Inhabitants, and preferving the Rights and Characters of every one according to their refpective Rank, and avoiding every Act which could occafion Diftrefs or Difcredit to us. On this Account we were, and continue fatisfied with Mr. Haftings. It is therefore incumbent on us to reprefent without Myftery, according to our Religion, a few of the Particulars of his wife Conduct, which we have feen and heard, as follows:—Mr. Haftings performed innumerable Benefits on all the Inhabitants of this Country, difapproved of Oppreffion towards any one, difplayed Kindnefs and diftinguifhing Marks of Credit to ancient Families; and, on an Interview with Crowds of Men of Rank and Refpect, carefully avoided the Omiffion of any Inftance of Civility or Honour. He was not, in the Tranfaction of the Affairs of Revenue or Government, covetous of the Money or Property of any one, but kept the Farmers and Overfeers from committing Oppreffion. During his Adminiftration, this Country experienced

no

no Warfare or Commotion ; no Injury happened to the Property of any one ; on the contrary, every one enjoyed Peace and Security, and
Courts of Civil and Criminal Jurisdiction were
firmly eftablifhed, by which our Lives and Property were protected from Thieves and Plun-
derers, and we were guarded from the Irrup-
tions of the Hill People, with which this Country was frequently over-run and deftroyed. He
permitted the free Force of our own Laws of
Relation ; he exerted every Nerve in the Cultivation of the Country, and tranfacted the Affairs of Government and Finance uprightly, and
with Juftice ; and not entertaining in his Difpofition the leaft Share of Haughtinefs, he laboured at our Eafe and Profperity. By thefe Means,
the Name and Authority of the King and Company of England were fo eftablifhed during his
Government, throughout all Hindoftan, that no
one could venture to raife the Head of Rebel-
lion. In fhort, Mr. Haftings poffeffed every
good Quality, and was well verfed in the Manners and Cuftoms of this Country, and always
exerted himfelf in the Prefervation of our Religion and Characters. On this Account we,
Inhabitants of thefe Diftricts, were happy during his Government, and are highly fatisfied
and pleafed with him.

The Seals and Signatures to this Addrefs, 43.

Under the Seals and Signatures as under written.

All we Zemindars, Choudries, and Talookdars, of the Diftrict of Akbarnagur, commonly
called Raje Mhal, in the Kingdom of Bengal,
have

have heard that the Gentlemen in England are
displeased with Mr. Haftings on Sufpicion that
he oppreffed us, Inhabitants of this Place, took
our Money by Deceit and Force, and ruined the
Country ;—Therefore we, upon the Strength of
our Religion, and religious Tenets, which we
hold as a Duty upon us, and in order to act
conformable to the Decrees of God in delivering Evidence, relate the praife-worthy Actions,
full of Prudence and Rectitude, Friendship and
Politeness, of Mr. Haftings, poffeffed of great
Abilities and Underftanding ; and by reprefenting Facts, remove the Doubts that have
poffeffed the Minds of the Gentlemen in England : That Mr. Haftings diftributed Protection
and Security to Religion, and Kindnefs and
Peace to us all. He is free from the Charge of
Embezzlements and Fraud, and that his Heart
is void of Covetoufnefs and Avidity. During
the Period of his Government no one experienced from him other than Protection and
Juftice, never having felt Hardfhips from him ;
nor did the Poor ever know the Weight of an
oppreffive Hand from him. Our Characters and
Reputations have always been guarded in Quiet
from Attack by the Vigilance of his Prudence
and Forefight, and preferved by the Terror of
his Juftice. He never omitted the fmalleft
Inftance of Kindnefs and Goodnefs towards us
and thofe entitled to it, but always applied, by
Soothings and Mildnefs, the Salve of Comfort
to the Wounds of Affliction, not allowing a
fingle Perfon to be overpowered by Defpair.
He difplayed his Friendfhip and Kindnefs to all.
He deftroyed the Powers of the Enemies and
wicked Men by the Strength of his Terror.

K   'He

He tied the Hands of Tyrants and Oppreffors by his Juftice, and by this Conduct he fecured Happinefs and Joy to us. He re-eftablifhed the Foundation of Juftice, and we at all Times, during his Government, lived in Comfort, and paffed our Days in Peace. We are many, many of us fatisfied and pleafed with him. As Mr. Haftings was perfectly well acquainted with the Manners and Cuftoms of thefe Countries, he was always defirous of performing that which would tend to the Prefervation of our Religion, and of the Duties of our Sects, and guard the religious Cuftoms of each from the Effects of Misfortunes and Accidents. In every Senfe he treated us with Attention and Refpect.—We have reprefented without Deceit what we have ourfelves feen, and the Facts that happened from him. .

The Seals and Signatures to this Addrefs, 54.

Under the Names as under-written.

We, Inhabitants of the Hills in Ingleterry, in the Chuckla of Rajemhal and Boglepore, have learnt that the Inhabitants of the Diftrict of Boglepore have written in Praife of Mr. Haftings, wherefore why fhould not we, who are praifing Mr. Haftings, write alfo, and not remain filent? We therefore reprefent, that we formerly lived in the Hills, like the Beafts of the Forefts, and during the Government of Mr. Haftings became like other Men, and the Qualities and Honours of Men were inftilled into us. Formerly our Means of Subfiftence were no other than thofe of Plunder and Rapine, and we exifted with the greateft Difficulty; but

now,

now, by the wife Conduct of that Gentleman, we live at Eafe, and, like others, are happy and fatisfied with the Company. As this Eafe and Civilization, which has produced Refpect to us among Mankind, has been the Effect of Mr. Haftings's Conduct and Management, we have never experienced other than Kindnefs, nor have any one of us heard of any Oppreffion from him; on this Account we are pleafed with Mr. Haftings.

The Names to this Addrefs, 47.

Copy Letter from the acting Judge of Patna—tranfmitting a Perfian Addrefs from that City; alfo Copy of Two Letters from the Deputy Perfian Tranflator.

To Edward Hay, Efquire, Secretary to the Government at Fort William.

Sir,

I WAS favoured with your Letter of the 31ft March laft; and a Sooruthat refpecting Mr. Haftings having been fent to me by the principal Inhabitants of this City, I now do myfelf the Honour to tranfmit it to you.

I am, Sir,
Your moft obedient
Patna Dewanny   humble Servant,
Adaulut, 3d   (Signed) H. DOUGLAS,
Sept' 1788.   Act' Judge.

A true Copy.
E. Hay,
Sec' to the Gov'.

K 2   To

To Edward Hay, Esquire, Secretary to the Government.

Sir,

. In my Letter of Yesterday's Date, accompanying further Advices relative to Mr. Hastings, in order to preserve the List of them regular, I inserted under the Letter Z, an Address from the Inhabitants of Patna, with Translation, which was not completed, the Names to it not being made into English. The Translation of them is now in hand; but from the Number and confused Order of the Seals and Signatures annexed to it, I shall not be able to prepare it to fill the Place allotted it in the above-mentioned Letter, to go by the Packet of the William Pitt; I therefore request you will annex this Letter to that of Yesterday's Date, in order to explain the Cause that the Patna Address does not accompany according to the List, and that it may be deferred until the next Dispatch to England.

I am, Sir,

Your most obedient

Calcutta,   humble Servant,

5th Nov' 1788. (Signed) G. F. CHERRY,

D. P. T'ₜ

A true Copy.

E. Hay,

Secr' to the Gov'.

To Edward Hay, Esquire, Secretary to the Government.

Sir,

Having, under Date 5th November last, been under the Necessity of withholding the Address

from

from the Inhabitants of Patna, marked in my
Letter of the 4th November with the Letter
Z, for Reasons already assigned, I have now the
Pleasure to forward you the original Address
from Patna, with a Translation thereof, under
the same Mark as in the List accompanying my
Letter of the 4th November.

I now forward you sundry other Addresses received since my last, from the Vakeels of the several Zemindars, &c. with Translations of the
same, according to a List accompanying.

    I am, Sir,
     Your most obedient Servant,
  Calcutta, (Signed) G. F. CHERRY.
22d Decʳ 1788.   D. P. Tʳ.

  A true Copy.
    E. Hay,
   Secʳ. to the Govʳ.

Z.

Translation of a Persian Address from the Inhabitants of Patna.

*Translation of an Address relative to Mr. Hastings,
under the Seals and Signatures of the Inhabitants
of the City of Patna.*

IT having come to the Hearing of all us
 Men, both high and low, of every Sect and
Persuasion, as well Hindoos as Mahomedans,
the Inhabitants and Natives of the City of Pat-
            na,

na, Part of the Territories belonging to the
Dewanny of the Englifh Company, that the
Gentlemen of England are difpleafed with the
late Governor General, Warren Haftings, upon
the Sufpicion that exercifing Tyranny and Oppreffion, and taking from us, by Artifice, and
Fraud, and Force, our Property, he laid wafte
the Country; we therefore, according to the
Dictates of our feveral Religions and facred Ordinances, which we hold to be ftrictly binding
on our Confciences, and in Obfervance alfo of
that Divine Precept, " Bear ye Teftimony,"
do thus publifh a true Account of the Nature
and Circumftances of the Conduct of Mr. Haftings, an honoured Perfonage of efteemed Qualities, who was perfect in Caution and Rectitude, complete in Virtue and Benevolence, and
firft amongft thofe Characters who are figna-
lized by their great Harmony and Wifdom,
and was honoured both by the Kings of Hindoftan and England; and by thus giving Ut-
terance to the Words of Truth and Juftice,
cleanfe the Mirrours of the Hearts of the Gentlemen of England from the Ruft of Sufpicion.
This Perfon is clothed with Probity and Religion as with a Garment, and is adorned by the
Protection of the People, and the Prefervation
of us the Worfhippers of God, as it were with
a Jewel; the Skirt of his Exiftence is unfullied
by the Stain of Difhonefty or Prejudice, and the
Mirrour of his Heart is unclouded by the Duft
of Avarice. In the Time of his Government,
and during the Period of his Adminiftration,
no one has feen in him any Thing but the Protection of the Subjects, and the Difpenfation of
Juftice;

Juftice; never did the Dirt of Affliction feat it-
felf through him on the Hearts of the People,
nor did he ever break the Glafs like Minds of
the lowly with the Stone of Violence. As an
Army is kept in Safety by its Watch Guards, fo
he protected the Honours of Strangers and
Natives by his Vigilance and Forefight, and
kept them defended in the Caftle of Security
from the Troops of Adverfity. The Sanctuary
of the Welfare of us humble Men was preferved
in Safety by the fuperintending Care of his
Juftice and Benevolence; he did not omit the
fmalleft Particle of Friendfhip towards us, and
towards whoever elfe were deferving of it, but
always by kind Words and benign Acts adminiftered the Balm of Comfort to the wounded
Hearts of the Afflicted. He left not One of
us all, not a fingle Individual, to be melted in
the Crucible of Defpair. In his compaffionate
Nature and great Kindnefs he favoured us all.
The Feet of the Endeavours of wicked Men
were broken by the Axe of his Awe, and the
oppreffive Hands of Evil Doers were bound by
the ftrong Cords of his Juftice. By thefe Means
the Doors of Happinefs and Delight were opened
to us. He new laid the Foundations of Juftice
and the Pillars of the Law. In every Shape we
the Inhabitants of this Country, during the
Time of his Adminiftration, lived in Eafe and
in Peace. We are therefore greatly fatisfied
with and thankful to him. As the faid Mr.
Haftings was long acquainted with the Modes
of Government in thofe Regions, fo the inmoft
Purpofe of his Heart was openly and fecretly,
in Word and in Deed, bent upon all thofe
Things which might maintain inviolate our Religions,

ligions, Ordinances, and Perſuaſions, and guard us in every the minuteſt Reſpect from Misfortune and Calamity. In every Way he cheriſhed us in Honour and Credit. Whatever we have in our own Perſons really experienced from him, and whatever has been clearly manifeſted by him, and whatever has been clearly, we have for the Sake and in the Name of God, without the Arts of Hypocriſy, truly and juſtly thus declared. In this there is no Doubt.

Seals and Signatures to the above Addreſs.

KAUZIES*.

Moolah Hurreat Ullah Khaun Wauyer, the chief Kauzy.

Kauzy Sujed Ameen U Deen.

Under this Seal is written, A Supporter of Students, the Son of Kyaut Muzzeid, who was the Son of Shurreef Udeen, Proprietor of the Village Birtooly, in the Purgannah of Rotas, by the Mother's Side, Grandſon of the Kauzy Shooker Ullah, who was the Son of Cauzy Peer Mahommud, the Hereditary Kauzy of the Purgunnah of Kauter, in the Sircar of Bahar. This Subſcriber is alſo Naib of the Kauzy of the Fouzdar of the Diſtrict of Patna, in the Soubeh of Behar.

* N. B. The Titles on many of the Seals are very numerous.—In the Tranſlation it has been thought neceſſary to retain only the moſt familiar.

Kauzy

Kauzy Subghut Ullah.

Under this Seal is written, - The Contents of this Paper are strictly true; Kauzy of the Purguhnah of Burragong, and Boonea, and Punwaurah, in the Sircar of Shawabad, in Behar.

MOOFTIES.

Moofty Sujed Ibrahim Hofein.
Under this Seal is written, " Fact."
Moofty Doft Mahommed.
Under this Seal is written, " Fact."
Moofty Sujed Fuzl Ullah.
Under this Seal is written, " Fact."
Moofty Sheikh Muffy Oolah.
Under this Seal is written, " Fact."
Moofty Sujed Mohummed Hofein.
Under this Seal is written, " In Truth, Mr.
" Haftings was famous and celebrated for
" his Goodnefs."

Suddaurut Punnah, i. e. Officers appointed by the Crown to fuperintend the Charity Lands.

Zein U Dein Ally Hyder Khawn.
Under this Seal is written, " The Seal of
" the Sudder of the Sobah of Bahar;
" whatever is written in this Paper is
" ftrictly true."
Sujed Wully Allum, Motehurully or Procurator appointed by the Englifh Government for the Purpofe of fuperintending the Intereft of

L   thofe

thofe holding Charity Lands in the Diftrict of Bahar.

CANOONGOES.

Roy Bulwunt Sing.
    Under this Seal is written, " Roy Bulwunt
    " Sing, Canoongoe of the Sudder of the
    " Soubah Bahar, and an immediate Ser-
    " vant under the Emperor, bears Tefti-
    " mony of the Truth of this Paper."

Abdhoo Peim Chund.
    Under this Seal is written, " Peim Chund, a
    " Servant of the Emperor, a Mohurrer of
    " Roy Bulwunt Sing, and of Roy Purfud
    " Ram, Canoongoes of the Sudder of Ba-
    " har."

Roy Nirmul Sing, Son of Purrein Sing.
    Under this Seal is written, " Roy Nirmul
    " Sing, the Canoongoe of the Sudder of
    " Bahar, bears Teftimony to the Truth of
    " this Paper."

Sittaram Sahoy.
    Under the Seal is written, " Sittaram, the
    " Gomaftah of Roy Nirmul Sing, the
    " Canoongoe of the Sudder of Bahar, is
    " perfectly and fatisfied."

Roy Perfudram.
    Under the Seal is written, " Roy Perfudram,
    " an immediate Servant of the Emperor,
    " and Canoongoe of the Sudder Bahar,
    " bears Teftimony to the Truth of this
    " Paper."

Akund Sing.
    Under this Seal is written, " The Seal of
    " Akund Sing, the Canongoe of the Sud-
13   " der

" der of the Purgunnah of Ball, &c. in
" Sircar Sarun."

The Signature of Khemajeet Roy, the Canon-
goe of the Purgunnah of Milkie and Boofau-
ry, in the Sircar of Harjee Poor, belonging
to Bahar, by the Pen of Behadre Sing, the
Deputy of the faid Canoongoe.

The Signature of Roy Anoop Loll and of Rou-
ſhun Loll, Canoongoes of the Purgunnah of
Milkie, in the Sircar of Haujy Poor, belonging to Bahar, by the Pen of Behadre Sing,
Deputy of the faid Canoongoe.

Ram Sahoy Heim Sing.
Under the Seal is written, The Signature and
Seal of Heim Sing, the Canoongoe of the
Purgunnah of Noubut Poor Bullea, in the
Soubah of Bahar.

Rogonaut Sahoy.
Under the Seal is written, The Signature and
Seal of Rogonaut Sahoy, the Grandſon of
Kiſhen dew Doſs, and the Canoongoe of
the Purgunnah of Soroo, in the Sircar of
Shawabad, in Bahar.

Bhekun Loll.
Under the Seal is written, The Signature of
Bhekun Loll, the Gomaſtah of Roy Perſud
Ram, and Roy Nulwut Ram, the Canoon-
goe of the Sudder of the Soubah of Bahar.

Nuſſurrut Ally.
Under the Seal is written, The Signature
of the Canoongoe of the Purgunnah of
Saundeh.

The Signature of Behadre Ally, the Servant of
the Emperor, the Canoongoe of the Purgunnah and City of Azeemabad, in the
Sircar and Soubah of Azeemabad.——

Under

Under the Juftice of Mr. Haftings I was happy.

The Signature of Odey Chund, the Gomaftah of Sheikh Behadre Ally, Canoongoe of the Pergunnah of Azeemabad.

The Signature of Bowanny Sing, a Servant of the Emperor, and a Canoongoe of the Pergunnah and City of Azeemabad, in the Sircar and Soubah of Bahar.—In the Juftice of Mr. Haftings I was pleafed and happy.

The Signature of Kifhun Chund, the Gomaftah of Bowany Sing, and Canoongoe of the Pergunnah Haveylee of Azeemabad.

The Signature of Bolaunut, a Servant of the Emperor, and a Canoongoe of the Pergunnah and City of Haveyley Azeemabad.—In the Time of Mr. Haftings I was happy, in a State of perfect Eafe.

Doorgah Sahoi, the Gomaftah of Bolonaut Canoongoe.

Omrahs, and the Sons of Omrahs, Khawns, Munfubdars, and Zemeendars, being Mahomedans.

Moneer ul Molk Moneer ul Dowlah Khawn Zummaun Khawn Behadre Nadir Jung.
Under the Seal is written, In doing good to Mankind Mr. Haftings had no equal.

Mahommed Moftekeem Khawn.
Under this Seal is written, Mohummed Moftekeem Khawn, Son of the Nawaub Mozuffer Khawn, who was the Nephew of the Ameer ul Amrah Nabob Sumfaum ul Dowlah Khaundowran Behadre, who was the Chief Bofhy of all Hindoftan.

Mahommed Khawn Behadre ul Molk Delawurzung.

Under

Under the Seal is written; The Son-in-law
of the Nawaub Moneer ul Dowlah Reiza
Kooley Khan. Behadre Nadir Jung.

Sujed Mohummed Khawn.

Under his Seal is written, Sujed Mohummed
Khawn, the Grandfon of the Nawaub Mo-
reed Khawn, deceafed.

Himmut Khawn Behadre.

Under his Seal is written, Grandfon of the
Nawaub Azum Khawn Azum ul Dowlah
Shumfheer Jung Behadre, who was the
Son of the Nawaub Mufleh udeen Khaun
Mufleh O Dowla Behadre.

Sujed Lutf Ally Khawn.

Under his Seal is written, I, the humbleft of
the Servants of God, am a Grandfon of the
Nawaub Azum Khawn Azum U Dowlah
Shumfheer Jung Behadre, and the Son of Sujed Ameer Mohummed Khawn Behadre.—
I affirm, fwearing by the Prophet, and by
the holy Fathers, upon all of whom be the
Grace of God, that without ever having
feen Mr. Haftings, I am thankful to him.
—In Truth, that excellent Gentleman was
without an Equal.—Even in former Times,
there were few Rulers fo juft, and poffeffed
of fuch Liberality, that all Mankind, from
the high to the low, from the great to the
fmall, fhould, on all Accounts, be thankful to him ; that not one Individual of the
whole human Race fhould complain of
him.—God is Witnefs, that the late Governor General is one of thofe Rulers
who are of diftinguifhed Eminence. Where-
ever he is, may God preferve him under
his holy Care and Protection.

Sujed

Sujed Sheer Ally Khawn Behadre.

> Under his Seal is written, Sujeed Sheer Ally
> Khawn, Son of Sujed Mohummed Kofeen
> Khawn Behadre, who was the Son-in-law of
> Sujed Abdul Ally Khawn Behadre Shujah
> Jung.

Abdul Huffun Khawn.

> Under his Seal is written, The Son of the
> Nawaub Himmut Khawn.

Hofein Ally Khawn.

> Under his Seal is written, The Grandfon
> of Salim Ally Khawn, deceafed, and the
> Nephew of Kulb Ally Khawn, deceafed,
> Daroga of the Adawlut of the Soubah Bahar.

Ally Azeem Khawn Behadre.

> Under his Seal is written, Ally Azeem
> Khawn, the Zemindar of the Sircar of
> Gauzipoor, in the Soubah of Allahabad,
> and Proprietor of Lands in the Soubah
> of Bahar.—I am perfectly fatisfied with,
> and grateful to Mr. Haftings. I hereunto
> affixed my Seal the 2d of Jummady ul
> Omrah, in the Fuffily Year 1195.

Meerza Abdoola.

> Under his Seal, Meerza Abdoola, the Son of
> Kulb Ally Khawn, who was the Son of
> Ally Cooly Khawn.

Wully ooalla Khawn.

> Under his Seal is written, Wully oolla Khawn,
> a Servant of the Emperor, a Jageerdar, is
> the Son of Gholaum Imaum a Dein Khawn,
> deceafed, who was the Sifter's Son of the
> Nawob Ahumed Khawn, deceafed.—What
> is written in the Text is exempt from all
> Doubt.

Mohummed Mukkeem Khawn.

> Under his Seal is written, There is no Doubt
> in

in the above. In all that concerned Mankind, he was without an Equal.

Wahed Ally Beig.

   Under his Seal is written, Wahed Ally
   Beig Khawn, Ameen of the Soubah of Behar, bears Teftimony to this.

Sujed Abafs Ally Khawn Ruzvy.

   Under this Seal is written, Son of Sujed
   Affud Ally Khawn, deceafed, who was the
   Son-in-law of Suraj ul Dowla, deceafed.——
   In truth, he (Mr. Haftings) was a Man of
   Underftanding, and worthy of governing.

Anal Greeb.

   Under his Seal is written, Well known by
   the Name of Sujed Fuzl oola Khawn
   Hofeiny.

Mohummed Ally Khawn.

   Under his Seal is written, Mohummed Ally
   Khawn, the Daroga of the Foujedary
   Adawlut for the Diftrict of Azeemabad,
   and Soubah of Bahar, bears Teftimony to
   this Paper.——The Contents of the Text are
   true.

Sujed Ifmaeel Ally Khawn Behadre.

   Under this Seal is written, Sujed Ifmaul
   Ally Khawn, the Son of Sujed Abdul Ally
   Khawn Behadre Shuja Jung, who was the
   Brother's Son of the Nawob Izut Khawn,
   the Soubehdar of Azeemabad.

Mohummud Ally Khawn.

   Under this Seal is written, Mohummud Ally
   Kawn, the Son of Khadim Hofein Khawn.

Aboo Tooraub Kawn.

   Under this Seal is written, Palpably true.
   Aboo Tooraub Khawn is the Son of Abul
   Coffim Khawn, deceafed.

Hedayet Hofein Khawn.

                 Under

Under this Seal is written, Thank God for
all Things—I have seen the Truth of what
is written in this Paper.

Erſhaud Khawn.

Under this Seal is written, Erſhaud Khawn,
the Son of the Nawaub Ameen ul Dowlah
Behadre.

Sujed Hyder Ally Khawn.

Under this Seal is written, So long as Mr.
Haſtings was Governor of the Soubah of
Bengal, &c. no Evils reached me ; on the
contrary, I continued in perfect Eaſe.

Mohummed Beig Khawn.

Under his Seal is written, The Son of Meer
Meyer Ally Khawn.

Mohummed Reeza Khawn.

Under this Seal is written, Mohummed Reza
Khawn, the Son-in-law of Abul Coſſim
Khawn, deceaſed.—There is no Doubt of
the Juſtice and Equity of Mr, Haſtings.

Hardy Ally Khawn, Phyſician.

Nuuwauſiſh Hoſein Khawn.

Under this Seal is written, Evidently true.
Nuuwauſiſh Hoſein Khawn, the Grandſon
of Abul Coſſim Khawn, deceaſed.

Nuuwauſiſh Huſſun Khawn.

Evidently true. Nuwauſiſh Huſſun Khawn,
the Grandſon of Abul Coſſim Khawn, deceaſed.

Ghawzy u Deen Ally Khawn.

Under this Seal is written, Evidently true.

Biſmilla Khawn.

Under this Seal is written, There is no Doubt
of this.

Abkarkhaun Behadre.

Under this Seal is written, Mr. Haſtings was
the Benefactor of Mankind, and in every
Thing

Thing worthy of a Ruler was without an
Equal. I am a Munſubdar of the Emperor.

Hafiz Ghwolaum Ally Khawn, Munſubdar of
the Empire.

Mohummed Khawn, Fedvy Shah Allum Bad-
ſhahy Gauzy.

Under this Seal is written, The Son of Fayez
Ally Khawn, deceaſed, who was the Bok-
ſhy and Naib of the Soubah of Azeemabad under Mohaubut Jung.—I ſwear by
my God and my Prophet, that during the
Time of Mr. Haſtings's Government I
lived in perfeƈt Peace, and that I was much
concerned at his Departure.

Mohummud Aſkurry Khawn.

Under his Seal is written, The Grandſon of
Fayez Ally Khan, deceaſed, the Bohſhy of
Nawob Mohaubut Jung.

Mohummud Ally Khawn.

Under his Seal is written, In proteƈting the
Subjeƈts, and in whatever was worthy of a
Chief, he was unequalled.

Mohummed Tucky Khawn Behadre.

Under his Seal is written, In proteƈting the
Subjeƈts, and in whatever was worthy of a
Chief, he was unequalled.

Mohummed Yâr Khawn.

Under this Seal is written, It is palpably
true, and I am ſatisfied and thankful.

Ally Zamin Khawn.

Under this Seal is written, He was a juſt
Man.

Huſſun Ally Khawn.

Under this Seal is written, Palpably true.

Mauſoom Ally Khawn.

Under this Seal is written, Mr. Haſtings Behadre was a very juſt Man, a Proteƈtor of
M   the

the People, and a Benefactor of the Poor.
Mohummed Cooley Khawn.

Under this Seal is written, I was, and am
satisfied with, and thankful to him.
Meer Mohumed Takir Khawn.

Under this Seal is written, Mr. Haftings Behaudre—may God encreafe his Profperity
—was a Man of Juftice, and a Protector of
the Poor.—All Mankind are fatisfied with
and thankful to him; I alfo Meer Mohummed Takir Khawn, the Grandfon of
Nawob Akeedutmund Khawn Behadre, am
fatisfied with him, and thankful to him.
Rajah Yekbaul Ally Khawn Behadre.

Under his Seal is written, Rajah Yekbaul
Ally Khaun Behadre, the Son of Rajah
Kaumguar Kaun Mien, and Zemendar of
the Purgunnahs of Nurhot and Summoy,
&c. in the Sircar and Soubah of Bahar.
Ghwolaum Hofein Khaun.

Under this Seal is written, The Grandfon of
Murza Moyeen u Dein Khaun, deceafed.
Niffaur Hofein Khaun Hofeiny.

Under this Seal is written, Notoriously true.
Khulleel Beig Khaun.

Under this Seal is written, Notoriously true.
Buddy u Deen Mohummed Khaun.

Under this Seal is written, Son of Mohummed Khaun, deceafed, a Phyfician.—From
the Commencement of Mr. Haftings's Government I never experienced any Hardfhip.
Meer Ghwolaum Hofein Khaun.

Under this Seal is written, From the Commencement of Mr. Haftings's Government
I never experienced any Hardfhip.

Abdvo-

Abdvolahkaun.

Under this Seal is written, " It is ſtrictly
" true."

Sumſaum u Dein Khaun.

Under this Seal is written, " It is ſtrictly
" true."

Meet Mohummed Baker Khawn Behadre.

Under this Seal is written, In the Juſtice of
Haſtings, and in his Protection of the
People, we are all ſatisfied and thankful; and during the Time of his Government we led our Lives in great Tranquillity, and continued in Abundance,
inſomuch that the very Name of Oppreſ-
fion was not heard of.

Hyder Ally Khaun.

Under this Seal is written, There is no Doubt
in this. From the Commencement in his
Government till his Departure for Europe,
the Inhabitants and People of this Country always continued in Peace and Security,
and they pray for the King and Country.

B E G U M S, and other Women of
Rank.

Soubed U Niſſa Beegum.

Under this Seal is written, Daughter of the
Nawob Abdul Ally Khaun Behadre, Son
of the Nawob Sultaun Khaun Behadre, One
of the Nobles of Jehaugur, and the Wife
of Shah Ally Khaun.

Zaheeut ul Niſſau Beegum, Widow of Jullal u
Dein Hoſen Khaun, deceaſed.

Sahib ul Niſſau, Wife of Ahmed Ally Khaun.

The

The Widow of Meer Afkerry, dece^d...

Moofummaut Saulyhau,

    Under this Seal is written, Notorioufly true.

    The Seal of the Wife of Imaum Bokfh
    Kaun, the Son of Kawzy Thiffun Róza
    Khaun, dece^d.

Motihaulikaun of Rajah Sadoo Ram, dece^d.

    Under this Seal written, From the pru-
    dent Counfels and perfect Wifdom of Mr.
    Haftings Behadre, he was in Truth a Man
    of Juftice, and a Protector of the People.

Fatimah.   The World obtained its Deliver-
    ance by Fatimeh.

Noor Beeby : From "*poor Beeby*," i. e. The
    Light of a Woman, the World obtained
    its Redemption.

Motehaulikaun Auleh Hofein Khaun.

    Under this Seal is written, Notorioufly true.

Men of Learning and Wifdom, Prelates, and Defcendants of the Prophet.

Ghwolaum Huffun.

    Under this Seal is written, The Defcendant
    and Reprefentative of the dignified Shah
    Arzanny, the Model of the Followers of
    God, the Chief of thofe poffeffing Reli-
    gious Wifdom. May God fanctify his ho-
    noured Tomb!—The Contents of this
    Paper are ftrictly true.

Wauris Ally.

    Under this Seal is written, Witnefs Warris
    Ally, the Motehwully (Superintendant of
    the Charity Lands) in the Pergunnah of
    Ghyaus Poor, in the Sircar and Soubah of
    Bahar.

                                Burkut

Burkut Ullah Hofeiny.

Under this Seal is written, The Seal of the Daroga of the Cuſtoms of Arzeemabad.

Mohummed Fiez Riozoy Hofeiny.

Under this Seal is written, The Keeper of the Stone bearing the Impreſſion of the Foot-ſtep of the Prophet, near the Garden of Jaffier Khaun, and well known by the Name of Sujed Meer.

Tubbyeut ul Huck Hofeiny.

Under this Seal is written, The Supporter and Preceptor of Students, well known by the Name of Mefafir ul Hofeiny ul Behary.

Mowlavy Fiozl ullah unfaury Calendar Kadry.

Under this Seal is written, He (Mr. Haſtings) was in Truth a juſt Man.

Ghwolaum Hofeign Hofeiny.

Under this Seal is written, We People were and are always thankful to Mr. Haſtings; during his Time we ſuffered not the leaſt Hardſhip.

Abdul Wahaub.

Under this Seal is written, "Strictly true."

Fiozl Ally, of the Race of Gung Skukker (a famous Durveiſh).

Yaur Ahmed.

Under this Seal is written, "Palpably true."

Ahmuddy Mokhtaur.

Under this Seal is written, There is no Doubt in this.

Mutteahu Rehmaum Apfum ul Kuttetaim.

Under this Seal is written, There is no Doubt in this, Ahmud Ally.

Sheikh Mutteah U Rehmaun, Jemmutdaur un-der the Engliſh Government, a Native of Iſlamabad, Reader of the Khutlah on the

Part

Part of the King, and under the Fouzdar.
Meer Sufder Ally.

Under this Seal is written, There is no Doubt
in this ; and in the Conduct which becomes
a Chief he was unequalled.

Mohummed Afhruff.

Under this Seal is written, There is no Doubt
in this.

Suged Mohummed Taper.

Under this Seal is written, I the offending
Slave of God, Mohummed Tahir, am the
Son of Mohummed Hofein Hofeiny.—
The Contents of this Paper are strictly
true.

Huffun Ally.

Under this Seal is written, The Son-in-Law of
Salim Ally Khaun, deceafed, Darogah of
the Adaulut.

Sujed Meer Ally.

Under this Seal is written, It is univerfally
known that he was a Man of Juftice.

Sujed Burkaut Ally.

Under this Seal is written, It is notorioufly
true that he was a juft Man.

Mohummed Moez.

Under this Seal is written, Witnefs to the
Contents of this Paper.

Abu Mohummed.

Under this Seal is written, Whatever is written in the Body of this Paper is notor-
rioufly true.

Wauris Ally.

Under this Seal is written, Palpably true.

Sujed Kulb Ally.

Under this Seal is written, I Sujed Kulb Ally,
the Son of a Prelate, and a Native of Guija,
bear

bear this Teſtimony, that a Perſon ſo endowed with all laudable Qualities, never before came from the Country of the Frungs. All Virtues which are proper for the Nature of Man were conſpicuous in him.

Azeem Ullah.

Under this Seal is written, A Prelate in the Soubah of Bahar.

Naſir Ally.

Under this Seal is written, I bear Teſtimony to the Truth of this, that a Perſon ſo endowed with all laudable Qualities never before came from the Country of the Frungs. All the Virtues which are neceſſary to the Nature of Man were conſpicuous in him.

Ghwolaum Neamut.

Under this Seal is written, Palpably true.

Mohil Ally.

Under this Seal is written, Witneſs Mohil Ally, an Amehdar of the Pergunnah Ghyauz Poor.

Sujed Shaw Alum, a Prelate.

Munooar Ally.

Under this Seal is written, God knows and beholds this.

Meer Coſſim Ally.

Under this Seal is written, There is no Doubt of this, that he was a Man of Juſtice. I am the Son of Meer Nuſſur Ullah.

Sujed Sufder Ally.

Under this Seal is written, So long as Mr. Haſtings Behadre was the Governor of the Subah of Bengal, &c. on no account did any Hardſhip befall me ; on the contrary, I remained in perfect Eaſe.

I   Meer

Meer Hoseiny, the Son of Meer Meyher Ally Khaun.

Meer Mahommed Hosein.

Under this Seal is written, The Seal of Meer Mahummed Hosein, a Merchant.

Sullabut Khaun, the Son of Baukir Khaun.

Sheikh Mohummed Sullah.

Under this Seal is written, a Native of Lahore.

Mohummud Waufil.

Under this Seal is written, All Men are satisfied with, and grateful to, Mr. Hastings for his good Conduct—I know he studied the Good of the Company—to this I swear by God.

Mohummud Hosein.

Under this Seal is written, The Seal and Writing of Meer Mohummud Hussun, Merchant.

Meer Khier U Deen Hosein.

Under this Seal is written, The Son of Meer Moraud Ally, the Bokshy of the Nawob Ahtrarum U Dowlah Behadre, the Soubahdar of the Soubah of Azeemabad.

Shahab Ally.

Under this Seal is written, "Strictly true."

Fuzl Ally Shurreef.

Under this Seal is written, God knows and beholds.

Abdahoo Abdaloo Beig.

Under this Seal is written, "Strictly true."

Mohummud Shurruff.

Under this Seal is written, "Strictly true."

Meer Wauyez Ally.

Under this Seal is written, In the Protection of the People, and in the Conduct that becomes

comes a Chief, he was without an Equal.

Peer Mohummed.

Under this Seal is written, Strictly true.

Kauzim Hofein.

Under this Seal is written, Palpably true.

Ghwolaum Ally.

Under this Seal is written, Notorioufly true.

Sheikh Abdoolah,

Under this Seal is written, Notorioufly true.

Fehaum Udeen Mohummed, the Moohfhy of
the Cuftoms at Azeemabad.

Ghwolaum Mortizah.

Under this Seal is written, In his good Conduct, and perfect Wifdom, Mr. Haftings
Behadre was in Truth worthy of Government,

Ghwolaum Abdul Kader.

Under this Seal is written, He was indeed a
Man of Truth and Juftice.

Sujed Hidauejet Ullah.

Under this Seal is written, Notorioufly true.

Shah Mohumed Jaffer Ally.

Under this Seal is written, Notorioufly true.

Mohummed Meyhdy.

Under this Seal is written, Notorioufly true.

Roufhun Ally.

Under this Seal is written, Mr. Haftings Behadre was in Truth a Man of Juftice, and
a Protector of the People.

Kulb Ally Ruzwy.

Under this Seal is written, In this there is no
Doubt.

Sujed Ghwolaum Huffun.

Under this Seal is written, In this there is
no Doubt.

N

Sujed Fuz Ally.

Under this Seal is written, He was a juft
Man.

Mohummed Illahy Bokfh.

- Under this Seal is written, In this there is no
Doubt.

Alabdul Moofnil Mohummed Jaffer.

Under this Seal is written, We People are
entirely fatisfied with, and thankful to Mr.
Haftings, for his Juftice and Protection of
the People.

Mohummed Farook.

Under this Seal is written, The Nephew of
Choudry Abdul Ruffool, the Choudry of
Azemabad.

Hajee Mohummed Khâyim.

Under this Seal is written, Of the Juftice
and Equity of Mr. Haftings there is no
Doubt.

Abdahoo Mohummed Mullich.

Under this Seal is written, We are greatly fatisfied with, and thankful to Mr. Haftings,
for his Juftice, his Munificence to the
Poor, and his Protection of the People.

Mohummud Mehdy.

Under this Seal is written, There is no Doubt
or Queftion that Mr. Haftings was juft;
that he fupported the Needy; and that he
protected the People: We were fatisfied
and thankful.

Afghur Hofein Hofeiny.

Under this Seal is written, This is notorioufly true.

Meer Ghwolaum Shurruf.

Under this Seal is written, I never heard or
faw

faw that Mr. Haftings was guilty of Injuftice to any Man.

Rockun Ally Hofeiny.

Under this Seal is written, In Truth, he was
unequalled for the Protection of the People : Whoever petitioned him obtained his
Defire.

Umeer u Deen Hofein.

Under this Seal is written, Mr. Haftings was
a Man of Underftanding.

Mohummed Abid.

Under this Seal is written, Mr. Haftings Behadre was, in the Protection of the People,
and in the Improvement of the Country, a
Ruler without an Equal : During the Time
of that Gentleman's Government I was
pleafed and happy.

Meer Inaut Ullah Hummandauny ut Hofeiny.

Under this Seal is written, Mr. Haftings was
in Juftice without a Second.

Ghwolaum Ally.

Under this Seal is written, This is notorioufly true.

Sujed Hummedauny Mohummudy ut Hofeiny.

Under this Seal is written, We were greatly
pleafed and fatisfied with Mr. Haftings for
his Juftice and for his Protection of the
People.

Sheikh Abdullah Moneyre.

Mr. Haftings Behadre was a juft Man, and a
Protector of the People, fo that in his Time
no Hardfhip was experienced.

Sheikh Barrullah Monery.

Mr. Haftings Behadre, in the Throne of Juftice and of Protection to the People, was
fuch a Man, that he has no Second.

Mohummed

Mohummed Sir Bolond.

    Under this Seal is written, It is notoriously true.

Sujed Burkut Ullah.

    Under this Seal is written, I call God to witness, that all Men were satisfied and happy during the Administration of Mr. Haftings, and that no Man fuffered any Hardships.

Meer Aha Ally Hofeiny.

    Under this Seal is written, From the Commencement of the English Company's Gonernment, a Man fo juft as Mr. Haftings has not come to this Country.

Sujed Muffech u Deen Hofein.

    Under this Seal is written, It is notoriously true.

Hufby Ullah.

    Under this Seal is written, I am a Witnefs to the Truth of this.

Meerza Lutf Ally Beig, bears Teftimony.

Sheikh Ghwolaum Mortiza, bears Teftimony.

Sheikh Boodun, bears Teftimony.

Meerza Bogul Beig, bears Teftimony.

Mortiza Kooly Beig, bears Teftimony.

Chumroo Khaun.

    Under this Seal is written, He was a Protector of the People, and a Difpenfer of Juftice.

Ghwolaum Mohummed.

    Under this Seal is written, I bear Teftimony to the Truth of this.

Eefo of Reza.

    Under this Seal is written, He was a Protector of the Poor, and a Difpenfer of Juftice to the People.

Ghwolaum Hofein.

    Under this Seal is written, It is notoriously true.   Sufdur

Sufdur Ally.

Under this Seal is written, It is notoriously true.

Sujed Rehmut Ullah.

Under this Seal is written, In this there is no Doubt.

Durveish Ally.

Under this Seal is written, Warren Haftings Behadre was famous for the Difpenfation of Juftice, and the Protection of the People. We, during the Period of his Government, were fatisfied, thankful, and at eafe.

Wauris Ally.

Under this Seal is written, In this there is no Deception.—I am a Rozenehdaur in the Sircar of Shahabad.

Sujed Nuzur Ally.

Under this Seal is written, The Contents are notoriously true.

Bundeh Durgahy.

Under this Seal is written, It is notoriously true.—I am the Naih Khaunfamann of the Nizamut in the Soubah of Bahar.

Khaujeh Jummaul, the Son of Hofein Bokfh.

Sujed Mahummed Aflem.

Under this Seal is written, The Juftice of Mr. Haftings Behadre, and Protection of the Poor, are as clear as the Sun.

Shah Meer Butchoo.

Under this Seal is written, As a juft Man he was without his like.

Durveifh Ally.

Under this Seal is written, I am Manager of Affairs for the Family of Meer Mohummud Humaum, who was the Son of Meer Mohummud Imaum Behary.

Darrifh

Darrifh Ally.

Under this Seal is written, It is true, that Mr. Haftings Behadre was fit for Government, and for the Difpenfation of Juftice.—We were fatisfied with and thankful to him.

Meer Shurruff u Deen Hofeiny.

Under this Seal is written, I, Meer Shurruff u Deen, am the Brother of Meer Afzul, the Uncle of Meer Afhroff, an Inhabitant of Patna, and a Dependant of the Eng-lifh Company Behadre. From the Juftice of Mr. Haftings, his Protection of the People, and his excellent Conduct towards them, the People of other Countries de-fired, as for Example, thofe of Cafhmeer lift up their Hands in Prayer, that God would make the Englifh Government the Lot of their Country.—Many People de-livered Petitions to him.

Sujed Waurzullah Hofeiny.

Under this Seal is written, The Son of Meer Noor u Deen, deceafed.—I fwear by the God of Kauba, that during the Time of Mr. Haftings I never fuffer any Hardfhip.

Nuffur Ullah.

Under this Seal is written, It is true.

Meer Noor Ullah.

Under this Seal is written, It is true.

Khaujeh Mohummed Muhfoot.

Under this Seal is written, It is notorioufly true. There is no Doubt or Queftion.— The Gomaftah of Khaujeh Summy.

Niffaur Ally.

Under this Seal is written, It is notorioufly true.

Ruffee

Ruffee u Deen Hofein.

Under this Seal is written, In this there is no
Deception.

Behadre Ally.

Under this Seal is written, It is ftrictly true.

Mohummed Roufham.

Under this Seal is written, Mr. Haftings was
a juft and equitable Man.

Sheikh Tauj u Deen.

Under this Seal is written, It is ftrictly true
that Mr. Haftings was a Man of Juftice,
and that I am greatly diftreffed by his Departure.

Meer Sujed Ally.

Under this Seal is written, Mr. Haftings Behadre, in the Bufinefs of protecting the
People, was a Ruler without an Equal.

Khajeh Nyam Ullah.

Without Doubt or Queftion he was a Man of
Juftice.

Rajahs and Roys, and Zemeendars and Civil
Officers, and other Perfons of Rank, being
Hindoos.

Roy Bunwaury Loll.

Under this Seal is writtten, I am the Nephew of Maha Rajah Ram Narain Behadre,
and of the Maha Rajah Deery Narain Behadre, Subahdars of the Soubah Bahar.
From the noble Generofity and the princely
Munificence of the Governor Mr. Haftings
Behadre I with great Gratitude continued
in the Management of the Affairs of my
faid Two honoured Relations, and in the
Adminiftration of Patna.

Rajah

Pajah Buffunt Ram.

Under this Seal is written, The Manager and
Reprefentative, on the Part of Maha Rajah
Narrain Behadre, the Sobehdar of the Sobeh of Azemabad, commonly called the
Sobeh of Bahar, am very greatly fatisfied
with, and thankful to Mr. Haftings for his
good Conduct.

Roy Sook Loil.

Under this Seal is written, The Nephew of
Maha Rajah Ramnarain Behadre, deceafed,
the Soubehdar of the Soubah of Azemabad, commonly called The Soubah of
Bahar.

Gunga Perfaud.

Under this Seal is written, The Seal of the
Brother of Rajah Buffunt Roy.

Hurry Sing.

Under this Seal is written, A Relation of the
Rajah Buffunt Ram Saheb.

Zorauwur Sing.

Under this Seal is written, a Relation of the
Rajah Buffunt Ram Saheb.

Sing.

Under this Seal is written, The Son-in-Law
of Roy Mohun Loll.

Himmut Behadre.

The Grandfon of Rajah Moorly Dhur.

Baboo Loll Sing Behadre.

Under this Seal is written, I, the Well-wifher
of the Company, am the Nephew of Rajah Moorley Dhur, the ancient Hircarrah
of the Soubah of Azemabad.

Shittaub Roy.

Under this Seal is written, The hereditary
Dewan of the Maha Rajah Druj Narrain
Behadre, Soubehdar of Azemabad.

9   Roy

Roy Ram Sahoy.

> Under this Seal is written, The Son of Rajah Noubur Roy, deceafed, the Soubehdar of the Soubah of Bahar, commonly called Azemabad.

Nadir Bokfh Choudry.

> Under this Seal is written, A Chowdry of Azemabad.

Denanaut.

> Under this Seal is written, Deenanaut, Vakeel of Maha Rajah Ruttun Behadre Shah, the Rajah of Neepaul.

Surrup Narain.

> Under this Seal is written, The Signature and Seal of Baboo Surup Narain Sing, Choudry of Sircar Sarung, in the Sobeh of Bahar.

Roy Bowany Sahoy.

> Under this Seal is written, In this there is no Deception.

Rajah Beer Koonwur Sing.

> Under this Seal is written, Rajah Beer Koonwur Sing, the Rajah of Sircar Chicumpaurun, in the Soubah of Bahar.

Surrupjeet Sing.

> Under this Seal is written, The Signature and Seal of Surrujeet Sing, the Choudry of the Purgunnah of Surrifah, in the Sircar of Hajee Poor, in the Soubeh of Bahar.

Rajah Bikhramajeet Sing.

> Under this Seal is written, The Signature of the Rajah of Sircar Shuwabad, in Soubeh of Bahar.

Atchunt Roy.

> Under this Seal is written, It is ftrictly true that Mr. Haftings was a juft Man, and a Protector of the People.

Noubut

Noubut Roy.

Under this Seal is written, I Noubut Roy, the Vakeel of Sujed Ghwolaun Hosein Khaun Behadre, know that there is no Doubt or Question as to the Justice of Mr. Hastings, his Protection of the People, or his Humanity to all Mankind. My Constituent with a thousand Tongues bestows Praises on the Government of Mr. Hastings, and his Protection of the People. My Constituent is entirely satisfied with Mr. Hastings, and prays for his Welfare. My Constituent is now residing at Hoseinabad, the Place of his Ultumghaw; were he here, his Seal would be affixed to this Paper.

Hirdeal Dofs.

Under his Seal is written, Hirdeall Dofs, Owner of the Village Ahooneh, in the Pergunnah of Beewung.—Mr. Hastings's Service of the Country, his Protection of the People, and his Endowments as a Ruler, are well known.

Jey Persaud.

Under this Seal is written, Jey Persaud, the humblest of God's Servants, am the Owner of the Village of Pryjooneh, in the Purgunnah of Ghyaug Poor.—It is clearer than the Sun that all Men were satisfied and thankful during Mr. Hastings's Administration, and I above all Men.

Juggernaut Sahoy Bohore Sing Roy.

Under this Seal is written, It is palpably true that no Man can be offended with a Person of so much Justice.

The Signature of Choudry Behary Loll, of the

Purgunnah

Purgunnah of Haveyley Azeemabad. During
the Adminiftration of Mr. Haftings we were
fatisfied and happy.

Afaulet Roy.

Under this Seal is written, The Seal of the
Son of the Rajah Sadooram.—Mr. Haftings was a juft Man, and a Protector of
the People.

Mahtaub Roy.

Under this Seal is written, It is notorioufly
true.

Cheit Roy Tehwuckooly.

Under this Seal is written, Surriftehdaur of
the Pay Office and of the Intelligence Offices of the Soubah of Bahar.—What is
written in the Body of this Paper is true.

Chein Sing.

Under this Seal is written, Chein Sing, the
Gomaftah of the Choudry of Haveyley A-
zeemabad, bears Teftimony.

Doorga Sahoy Heereeh Loll.

Under this Seal is written, The hereditary
Mohfuddy of the Dewry of the Sircar of
Mahah Rajah Ram Narain Behadre.

Hunnomaun Sahoy Bukhtawur Sing.

Under this Seal is written, The Vakeel of
Rajah Buffunt Ram Sahib.

Moojy Loll.

Under this Seal is written, A Servant of the
Rajah Buffunt Ram Sahib.

Shew Perfaud.

Under this Seal is written, Sheo Perfaud, a
Mohhfuddy of the Nawob Mehdy Ally
Khaun Behadre, the Naib of the Soubah of
Azeemabad.

Jungy

Jungy Loll.

Under this Seal is written, Jungy Loll, the hereditary Moonfhy for the Nizamut of the Soubeh of Bahar.

Muddun Gopaul Keidhoo Loll.

Under this Seal is written, An Inhabitant of Patna, and the Naib of the Vakeel of the Dutch Factory.

Hunfray.

Under this Seal is written, An Inhabitant of Patna, and the Vakeel of the Dutch Factory.

Surdaur Sing.

Under this Seal is written, The Seal of the Moonfhy of the Cuftom Houfe at Patna.

Aufy Ram Loll.

Under this Seal is written, The Vakeel of Baboo Surrupnarrain Sing.

Jou Loll.

Under this Seal is written, The Seal of Jou Loll, the Motefuddy of Rajah Bickra Majeit Sing, the Rajah of Shawabad.

Oomrou Sing.

Under this Seal is written, A writer of the Cuftom Houfe.

Jey Gopaul Sing.

Under this Seal is written, The Son of Lalla Bifhurn Sing.—Whatever is written in the Body of this Paper, is free from all Doubt.

Mendoo Loll.

Under this Seal is written, The Nephew of Lala Huns Ranj, the Vakeel of the Dutch Factory, and an Inhabitant of Patna.

Gunga Ram.

Under this Seal is written, In this there is no Deception.

Buffawunt

Buffawunt Loll.

The Son of Moonfhey Reonwaur Sing, dece³.
" It is notorioufly true,"

Himmut Sing.

Under this Seal is written, In upright Coun-
fels and in perfect Wifdom Mr. Haftings
was in Truth a Man of Juftice, and a Protector of the People.

Ram Diaul Sing, the Uncle of Sadoo Ram.

Nubkifhore, the Son of Peim Chund.
It is notorioufly true.

Madhoo Surrun Roy.

Under this Seal is written, He was a juft
Man.

Ram Perfaud Roy.

Under this Seal is written, Mr. Haftings was
a Gift of God in his Mercy to Mankind.—
I fuffered no Hardfhip.

Munnear Sing bears Teftimony, without Doubt
or Queftion he was a juft Man.

Kifhurn Sahoy.

Under this Seal is written, It is notorioufly
true.

Goor Govind Sahoy Gooperfaud Sing.

Under this Seal is written, It is notorioufly
true.

Jeywahir Mull.

It is notorioufly true.

Beneram.

Under this Seal is written, It is ftrictly true.
Mr. Haftings was a juft Man, and the
People are greatly concerned at his Depar-
ture.

BANKERS and MERCHANTS.

Bughwaun Dofs, Jeweller.
Gunfaum Dofs and Bifhun Dofs, Chief of the
   Druggifts.
Dhomy Sah, Jeweller.
Mooda, the Choudry of the Shroffs.
Mooty Loll.
   Under this Seal is written, Mooty Loll, the
   hereditary Treafurer of the Soubeh of
   Bahar.—Whatever is written in the Perfian
   Character in this Paper is true.
Munnoo Sing, the Gomaftah of the Chowdry
   of the Cloth-merchants.
Kookum Chund, Jeweller.
Jewun Chund, Jeweller.
Mooty Sahoo, Jeweller.
Jewun Dofs, Cloth-merchant.
Sohun Mull, Cloth-merchant.
Burrull, Cloth-merchant.
Suddaunund Miffer, Cloth-merchant.
Matraw Dofs, Cloth-merchant.
Ram Sahoy, Cloth-merchant.
Doomun Sing, Cloth-merchant.
Nundram, Cloth-merchant.
Loll Jee, Cloth-merchant.

   Befides the above, there are a few Seals which
are neither numbered or tranflated, the Im-
preffion being illegible.

A true Tranflation.

(Signed)   G. F. CHERRY,
            D. P. T'.

True Copies.
    E. Hay,
    Secr' to the Gov'.

To Edward Hay, Esquire, Secretary to the Government.

SIR,

In my Letter of Yefterday's Date, accompanying further Addreffes relative to Mr. Haftings, in order to preferve the Lift of them regular, I inferted under the Letter Z. an Addrefs from the Inhabitants of Patna, with Tranflation, which was not completed, the Names to it not being made into Englifh.——The Tranflation of them is now in hand; but from the Number, and confufed Order of the Seals and Signatures annexed to it, I fhall not be able to prepare it to fill the Place allotted for it in the abovementioned Letter, to go by the Packet of the William Pitt; I therefore requeft you will annex this Letter to that of Yefterday's Date, in order to explain the Caufe that the Patna Addrefs does not accompany according to the Lift, and that it may be deferred until the next Difpatch to England.

I am, Sir,

Calcutta,
5th Nov' 1788.

Your obedient Servant,

G. F. CHERRY,
D. P. Trans'.

Copy Letter from the Collector of
Dinagepore, dated 13th October; with
a Translation of a Persian Paper tranfmitted by him.

Edward Hay, Efquire, Secretary to the
Government.

SIR,

AT the Requeft of the Vakeel of the Zemindars and Talookdars in this Diftrict, I
tranfmit you the accompanying Perfian Paper,
containing Teftimonies relative to Mr. Haftings.

I am, Sir,
Dinagepore,   Your moft obedient
October 13th, 1788.   humble Servant,
(Signed)   G. HATCH,
Coll' Dinagepore.

A true Copy.
E. Hay,
Sec' to the Gov'.

*Paper tranfmitted by the Collector of Dinagepore;
received 19th October 1788, and tranflated
purfuant to an Order from the Governor General
in Council, dated 27th April 1788.*

We, the Zemindars, Chowdries, and Talookdars of Pergunnah Selberres, &c. Diftricts ap-
pertaining to the Zellah of Dinagepore, have
heard that the Gentlemen in England are difpleafed with Mr. Haftings, on Sufpicion that he
oppreffed us Inhabitants of this Place, took our
Money

Money by Deceit and Force, and ruined the
Country ;—Therefore we, upon the Strength
of our Religion and religious Tenets, which
we hold as a Duty upon us, and in order to act
conformable to the Decrees of God in delivering Evidence, relate the praise-worthy Actions,
full of Prudence and Rectitude, Friendship and
Politeness, of Mr. Haftings; possessed of great
Abilities and Understanding; and by representing Facts, remove the Doubts that have possessed
the Minds of the Gentlemen in England. That
Mr. Hafting distributed Protection and Security
to Religion, and Kindness and Peace to us all.
He is free from the Charge of Embezzlements
and Fraud, and his Heart is void of Covetousness and Avidity. During the Period of his
Government, no one experienced from him
other than Protection and Justice, never having
felt Hardships from him; nor did the Poor ever
know the Weight of an oppressive Hand from
him. Our Characters and Reputations have
been always guarded in Quiet from Attack by
the Vigilance of his Prudence and Foresight,
and preserved by the Terror of his Justice. He
never omitted the smallest Instance of Kindness
and Goodness towards us and those entitled to
it, but always applied, by Soothings and Mildness, the Salve of Comfort to the Wounds of
Affliction, not allowing a single Person to be
overpowered by Despair. He displayed his
Friendship and Kindness to all; he destroyed the
Powers of Enemies and wicked Men by the
Strength of his Terror; he tied the Hands of
Tyrants and Oppressors by his Justice, and by
this Conduct he secured Happiness and Joy to
us. He re-established the Foundation of Jus-

tice;

tice; and we at all Times during his Government lived in Comfort, and paſſed our Days in Peace. We are many, many of us ſatisfied and pleaſed with him. As Mr. Haſtings was perfectly well acquainted with the Manners and Cuſtoms of theſe Countries, he was always deſirous of performing that which would tend to the Preſervation of our Religion, and of the Duties of our Sects, and guarded the religious Cuſtoms of each from the Effects of Misfortunes and Accidents. In every Senſe he treated us with Attention and Reſpect. We have repreſented without Deceit what we have ourſelves ſeen, and the Facts that happened from him.

The Signatures to this Addreſs, 26

A true Tranſlation.

(Signed)   G. F. CHERRY,
                        D. P. Tr.

A true Copy.

E. Hay,
Secr to the Govt.

Tranflations of the Perfian Addreffes from the Rajah of Burdwan, and Zemindars of the 24 Pergunnahs, and from Pundits of the 24 Pergunnahs, prefented by their Vackeels.

f f.

Paper delivered by the Vakeel on the Part of the Rajah of Burdwan, and the Zemindars of the 24 Pergunnahs, and tranflated purfuant to an Order from the Governor General in Council, dated 27th April 1788.

Petition, under the Signature of Rajah Mullic, Vakeel, on the Part of the Rajah of Burdwan, Radachurn Roy, &c. Zemindar of the 24 Pergunnahs.

THE Maha Rajah Dherage Teez Chund Behader, Zemindar of Purgunnah Burdwan, &c. has tranfmitted an Addrefs relative to Mr. Haftings, under his own Seal, and the Signatures in Bengalefe of 157 Zemindars in the 24 Pergunnahs, with a Copy thereof, authenticated by the Cauzy; and another Addrefs from the Pundits of the 24 Pergunnahs, written in the Shanfcrit Language, with a Perfian Tranflation of it, in order that they may be fent to Europe; and hopes that your Lordfhip will be pleafed to order them to be tranflated, and tranfmit the Original and Tranflation to England.

A true Tranflation.
(Signed)   G. F. CHERRY,
D. P. T'.

A true Copy.
E. Hay,
Secr⁷ to the Fort.

f f.

Under the Seal of Maha Rajah Dherage Teez-hund Behader, Zemindar of Pergunnah Burd-wan, &c. and the Signatures of the Choudries and Talookdars of the 24 Pergunnahs, as under written.

In the fame Terms as the laft Addrefs.

The Signatures to this Addrefs,   158

g g.

Addrefs from the Pundits of the 24 Pergunnahs, under the Signatures as under written.

Mr. Haftings's Difpofition was adorned with the Jewel of Patience, Firmnefs, Clemency, and Courage, great Complacency and Politenefs. He enlightened the World by the Brightnefs of his Conduct, the Praifes of which are fung by all learned Men. The Minifters of England, on the Sufpicion that Mr. Haftings took Money by Force and Deceit from the Natives of this Country, and ruined the Country, are difpleafed with him;—We, Inhabitants of the Country under the Company's Dominions, having heard this, in order to remove this Reflection on him who adminiftered Juftice, and to wipe away the Cloud from the Minds of the People of England, reprefent the good Conduct he followed: —That in regard to Inhabitants of this Country, of high, middling, and low, all the Three Degrees, he maintained them in the enlightening Roads of Religion, and cherifhed them with

7   parental

parental Kindneſs, without Self-intereſt. He
raiſed the Credit of Tutors and Students in every
Learning, by treating with Reſpect every Branch
according to its Inſtructions and Science ; and
from having been long reſident in this Country,
he was well acquainted with the Nature of the
Government of it. During his Adminiſtration
in this Kingdom, the whole World felt no Uneaſineſs or Adverſity, preſerved the beaten Track
of their Concerns, and lived in Peace.—This
was the Caſe with every one.

The Signatures to this Addreſs,   25

A true Tranſlation.

(Signed)   G. F. CHERRY,
True Copies.   D. P. Tᵣ.
E. Hay,
Secry. to the Fort.

---

*Papers delivered by the Vakeels on the Part of the
Zemindar of Pergunnah Jeſſore, Mahmoud Shaby,
&c. and tranſlated purſuant to an Order from
Governor General in Council, dated 27th April
1788.*

Petition from the Vakeels of the Zemindars
of Jeſſore and Mahmoud Shahy.

AN Addreſs relative to Mr. Haſtings, under
the Signature of Serrikaunt Roy, Zemindar of Pergunnah Jeſſore, &c. and one under
the Seals and Signatures of the Choudries of
Mahmoud Shahy, and the Talookdars of Zellah Jeſſore, with Copies thereof, having been
tranſmitted to the Preſence, we hope that they
may be tranſlated by Order of Government,
and

and the Tranflation and Original forwarded to
Europe.

A true Tranflation.

(Signed) G. F. CHERRY.

D. P. T.

A true Copy.

E. Hay,

Sec. to the Fort.

Under the Signature of the Serrikaunt Roy,
Zemindar of Pergunnah Jofeefpore, &c.

I have heard that the Gentlemen in England
are difpleafed with Mr. Haftings, on Sufpicion
that he oppreffed us Inhabitants of this Place,
took our Money by Deceit and Force, and
ruined the Country;—Therefore we, upon the
Strength of our religious Tenets, which we
hold as a Duty upon us, and in order to act
conformable to the Decrees of God in delivering Evidence, relate the praife-worthy Actions,
full of Prudence and Rectitude, Friendfhip and
Politenefs, of Mr. Haftings, poffeffed of great
Abilities and Underftanding; and by reprefenting Facts, remove the Doubts that have poffeffed the Minds of the Gentlemen in England.
That Mr. Haftings diftributed Protection and
Sincerity to Religion, and Kindnefs and Peace
to us all. He is free from the Charge of Embezzlements and Fraud, and his Heart is void
of Covetoufnefs and Avidity. During the Period of his Government no one experienced from
him other than Protection and Juftice, never
having felt Hardfhips from him; nor did the
Poor ever know the Weight of an oppreffive
Hand from him. Our Characters and Reputations

tions have always been guarded in Quiet from Attack by the Vigilance of his Prudence and Foresight, and preserved by the Terror of his Justice. He never omitted the smallest Instance of Kindness and Goodness towards us and those entitled to it, but always applied, by Soothings and Mildness, the Salve of Comfort to the Wounds of Affliction, not allowing a single Person to be overpowered by Despair. He displayed his Friendship and Kindness to us all. He destroyed the Powers of Enemies and wicked Men by the Strength of his Terror. He tied the Hands of Tyrants and Oppressors by his Justice; and by this Conduct he secured Happiness and Joy to us. He re-established the Foundation of Justice; and we at all Times during his Government lived in Comfort, and passed our Days in Peace: We are many, many of us satisfied and pleased with him. As Mr. Hastings was perfectly well acquainted with the Manners' and Customs of these Countries, he was always desirous of performing that which would tend to the Preservation of our Religion, and of the Duties of our Sects, and guarded the religious Customs of each from the Effects of Misfortunes and Accidents. In every Sense he treated us with Attention and Respect.——We have represented without Deceit what we have ourselves seen, and the Facts that happened from him.

A true Translation.

(Signed) G. F. CHERRY,

D. P. T'.

A true Copy.

E. Hay,

Sec' to the Fort.

Under the Seals and Signatures of the Zemindars, Chowdries, and Talookdars of the Ma-
hals of Mahmoud Shahy and Zillah Jeffore.

We Zemindars, Chowdries, and Talookdars
of the Mahls of Mahmoud Shahy and Zellah
Jeffore, have heard that the Gentlemen in England are displeased with Mr. Haftings, on Sufpicion that he oppreffed us, Inhabitants of this
Place, took our Money by Deceit and Force,
and ruined the Country;—Therefore we, upon
the Strength of our Religion and religious Tenets, which we hold as a Duty upon us; and in
order to act conformable to the Decrees of God
in delivering Evidence, relate the praife-worthy
Actions, full of Prudence and Rectitude, Friendfhip and Politenefs, of Mr. Haftings, poffeffed
of great Abilities and Underftanding; and by
reprefenting Facts remove the Doubts that have
poffeffed the Minds of the Gentlemen in England. That Mr. Haftings diftributed Protection and Security to Religion, and Kindnefs and
Peace to us all. He is free from the Charge of
Embezzlements and Fraud, and his Heart is
void of Covetoufnefs and Avidity. During the
Period of his Government no one experienced
from him other than Protection and Juftice, never having felt Hardfhips from him; nor did
the Poor ever know the Weight of an oppreffive
Hand from him. Our Characters and Reputations have been always guarded in Quiet from
Attack by the Vigilance of his Prudence and
Forefight, and preferved by the Terror of his
Juftice. He never omitted the fmalleft Inftance
of

of Kindnefs and Goodnefs towards us and thofe entitled to it, but always applied, by Soothings and Mildnefs, the Salve of Comfort to the Wounds of Affliction, not allowing a fingle Perfon to be overpowered by Defpair. He difplayed his Friendfhip and Kindnefs to us all. He deftroyed the Powers of Enemies and wicked Men by the Strength of his Terror. He tied the Hands of Tyrants and Oppreffors by his Juftice; and by his Conduct he fecured Happinefs and Joy to us. He re-eftablifhed the Foundation of Juftice; and we at all Times, during his Government, lived in Comfort, and paffed our Days in Peace. We are many, many of us fatisfied and pleafed with him. As Mr. Haftings was perfectly well acquainted with the Manners and Cuftoms of thefe Countries, he was always defirous of performing that which would tend to the Prefervation of our Religion, and of the Duties of our Sects, and guarded the Religious Cuftoms of each from the Effects of Misfortunes and Accidents. In every Senfe he treated us with Attention and Refpect.—We have reprefented without Deceit what we have ourfelves feen, and the Facts that happened from him.

The Seals and Signatures to this Addrefs,   72.

  A true Tranflation.
    (Signed) G. F. CHERRY,
          D. P. T'.
 A true Copy.
    E. Hay,
   Secʸ to the Govᵗ.

Tranſlation of a Perſian Addreſs from the
Rajah of Tannah Bahar, in Cooch Bahar;
preſented by his Vakeel.

*Paper delivered by the Vackeel on the Part of the
Rajah Hurrindernarrain, Rajah of Tannah
Beyhar, &c. in Cooch Beyhar, and tranſlated
purſuant to an Order from the Governor General
in Council, dated 27th April 1788.*

Under the Seals and Signatures as written.

I Rajah Hurrindernarrain, Rajah of Tannah
Beyhar, in Cooch Behar, and other Servants
and Dependants on the ſaid Raje, whoſe Seals
are hereunto annexed, have heard that the Gentlemen in England are diſpleaſed with Mr. Haftings, on Suſpicion that he oppreſſed us Inhabitants of this Place, took our Money by Deceit
and Force, and ruined the Country;—Therefore we, upon the Strength of our Religion and
religious Tenets, which we hold as a Duty
upon us, and in order to act conformable to the
Decrees of God in delivering Evidence, relate
the praiſe-worthy Actions, full of Prudence and
Rectitude, Friendſhip and Politeneſs, of Mr,
Haſtings, poſſeſſed of great Abilities and Underſtanding; and by repreſenting Facts, remove
the Doubts that have poſſeſſed the Minds of the
Gentlemen in England. That Mr. Haſtings
diſtributed Protection and Security to Religion,
and Kindneſs and Peace to us all. He is free
from the Charge of Embezzlements and Fraud,
and his Heart is void of Covetouſneſs and Avidity. During the Period of his Government no
one

one experienced from him other than Protection
and Juftice, never having-felt Hardfhips from
him ; nor did the Poor ever know the Weight of
an oppreffive Hand from him. Our Charaǎers
and Reputations have been always guarded in
Quiet from Attack, by the Vigilance of his Prudence and Forefight, and preferved by the Terror of his Juftice. He never omitted the
fmalleft Inftance of Kindnefs and Goodnefs towards us and thofe entitled to it, but always applied, by Soothings and Mildnefs, the Salve of
Comfort to the Wounds of Affliǎion, not allowing a fingle Perfon to be overpowered by
Defpair. He difplayed his Friendfhip and
Kindnefs to all; he deftroyed the Powers of
Enemies and wicked Men by the Strength of
his Terror. He tied the Hands of Tyrants and
Oppreffors by his Juftice ; and by this Conduǎ
he fecured Happinefs and Joy to us. He re-
eftablifhed the Foundation of Juftice ; and we
at all Times during his Government lived in
Comfort, and paffed our Days in Peace. We
are many, many of us fatisfied and pleafed with
him. As Mr. Haftings was perfeǎly well acquainted with the Manners and Cuftoms of thefe
Countries, he was always defirous of performing
that which would tend to the Prefervation of our
Religion, and of the Duties of our Seǎs, and
guarded the religious Cuftoms of each from
the Effeǎs of Misfortunes and Accidents. In
every Senfe he treated us with Attention and
Refpeǎ.—We have reprefented without Deceit
what we have ourfelves feen, and the Faǎs that
happened from him.

Q 2   The

The Seals and Signatures to this Addrefs.

Maha Rajah Hurrinderain.

Maha Ranny, the Mother of Maha Raja Hurrinderain.

Serbanund Goffein, Superintendant of the Raje
Moaindnarain Koar.

Nazir Deo Jebundernarain Koar.

Coffinaut Khaufhnubbees, the Rajah's Dewan.

Suftidhur Dofs, Vakeel at Calcutta.

Kifhen Caunt Buckihy.

Bifhenperfaud Ameen.

Jankeram Sirma, Vackeel at Calcutta.

A true Tranflation.

(Signed) G. F. CHERRY,
D. P. T'.

A true Copy.

E. Hay,
Secr' to the Gov'.

Tranflation of a Perfian Addrefs from the
Ranny of Rajefhahy, and her Son Rajah
Ramkiffen—prefented by her Vakeel.

*Paper delivered by the Vakeel on the Part of Mahd
Ranny Bowanny, and Rajah Ramkiffen, her
adopted Son, Zemindar of Pergunnah Rajefhaby,
&c. and tranflated purfuant to an Order from the
Governor General in Council, dated 27th April
1788.*

Same as the foregoing Addrefs.

Under the Seals of Maha Ranny Bhowany, and
her adopted Son Rajah Ramkifhen, and
others, as underwritten.

The

The Seals and Signatures to this Addrefs.

Maha Ranny Bowanny.
Rajah Ramkifhen, adopted Son to the above.
Ramkifhen, Nien Chunder Serma, Naib of
Pergunnah Rajefhahy, &c.
Permanund Dofs, Vakeel of Pergunnah Raje-
fhahy, &c.
Ram Caunt, Seriftadar.

———————

Tranflation of a Perfian Addrefs from the
Canongoes, Zemindars, &c. of Midnapore, prefented by their Vakeels.

*Paper delivered by the Vakeel, on the Part of the
Cannongoes, Zemindars, Chowdries, and Talookdars of Chucla Midnapore, tranflated purfuant to an Order from the Governor General
in Council, dated 27th April 1788.*

Same as the foregoing Addrefs.

The Seals to this Addrefs, 17.

Tranflation of an Addrefs from the Canongoes, &c. &c. &c. of Sylhet, prefented
by the Collector.

S. S.

*Tranflation of a Perfian Addrefs delivered by the
Canoongoes, Zemindars, Chowdries, and Talookdars of Sylhet, to Mr. Willis, Collector of the Revenues of that Diftrict.*

WE the Servants of the Imperial Court, the
Canongoes, Zemindars, Chowdries, and
Talookdars of the Diftrict of Sylhet, a De-
pendancy of the Soubah of Bengal, that Paradife
of Nations, have heard that the Gentlemen of
England are difpleafed with Mr. Haftings, upon
a Sufpicion, that exercifing Tyranny and Oppreffion over us, he took our Money by Fraud
and Artifice, as well as by Force, and that by
Mifmanagement he laid wafte the Country. We,
hearing this, are much aftonifhed! For the Skill
and Knowledge of Mr. Haftings in the Conduct
of Bufinefs, and in managing the Affairs both
of Revenue and Government, are notorious
throughout all Bengal and Hindoftan. We for
our Parts can fay, that he never took from us,
humble Men, a fingle Daun or Dhyrrum by
Force or Oppreffion, or by Fraud or Artifice;
nor was his Difpofition in any Degree inclined
to Avarice and Covetoufnefs; on the contrary,
he fowed the Seeds of Kindnefs in the Fields
of the Hearts of all the Hufbandmen and Subjects,

jects, and from the Showers which fell from the
Clouds of his Benevolence and Generofity, he
made the Hearts of the Poor to flourifh like a
a Garden. By Law and the Difpenfation of
Juftice he improved the Country. From the
Sword of the Wicked, who delight in Sedition,
he protected us defencelefs People with the
Shield of his Beneficence; and during the Time
of his Adminiftration and Government we
paffed our Time in Eafe and Pleafure. As he
was from a very early Period acquainted with
the Ufages and Cuftoms of this Country, fo he
laboured to preferve inviolate the Honour, the
Faith, and the Religion of us all. For thefe
Reafons we, according to our Religion and Be-
lief, and in purfuance of that holy Precept
" *withhold not your Teftimony*," have truly and
juftly made this public Declaration.

The Signatures to this Addrefs,   102

Copy Letter from the acting Collector
of Moorfhedabad; with a Tranflation
of a Perfian Addrefs from the Zemindars of Rocunpore, &c. &c. tranfmitted by him.

To Edward Hay, Efquire, Secretary to the
Government.

Sir,

THE Zemindars and Talookdars under this
Collectorfhip have delivered to me a Perfian
Addrefs relative to Mr. Haftings, and an at-
tefted

tefted Copy of it ; with a Requeft, that I would
forward them to the Governor General in Council, in order that they might be tranfmitted to
the Court of Directors.—In compliance with
their Requifition, I have the Honour to fend
you the above-mentioned Perfian Papers, together with a Copy of the Application from the
Zemindars and Talookdars to me.

I have the Honour to be, Sir,
Your moft obedient humble Servant,
(Signed) JOHN FENDAL,
Act Coll.

Zillah Moorfhedabad,
the 5th November 1788.

A true Copy.
E. Hay,
Secr to the Fort.

*Petition of the Zemindars of Rockunpore, Lufh-
kerpore, Jebinguerpore, &c. under the Collectorfhip of Moorfhedabad.*

We, your Petitioners, the Zemindars, Talookdars, and Chowdries of the Lands under
the Collectorfhip of Moorfhedabad, have written, figned, and fealed a Paper in Praife of
Mr. Haftings, for the Difpatch of which to the
Prefidency we requeft that you will fend the
Original, with our Seals and Signatures, together with a Copy thereof, attefted by the Seal
of the Cauzey, to the Right Honourable the
Governor General in Council at Calcutta, and
petition in our Name that the Right Honourable the Governor General in Council will be

9   kind

kind enough to order a Tranflation to be made
of that Paper, and that the Original with the
Tranflate may be forwarded to the Honourable
the Court of Directors in England.—It is juft,
and we have petitioned it.

A true Tranflate.

(Signed) JN. FIR,
Afs^t.

A true Copy.
    E. Hay,
        Sec^y to the Fort.

Papers delivered by the Vazeel of the Zemindars of
Pergunnah Rokumpoor, Lufkerpore, Jehanquir-
pore, &c. all the Mhals of Zillah Moorfheda-
bad, and tranflated purfuant to an Order
from the Governor General in Council, dated
27 April 1788.

    Petition from the Zemindars of Purgunnah
    Rokempore, Lufkerpore, Jehanquier-
    pore, &c. all the Mhals of Zellah
    Moorfhedabad ; addreffed to the Col-
    lector.

We, the Zemindars, Talookdars, and Chowdries of Zellah Moorfhedabad, have written an
Addrefs on the Virtues of Mr. Haftings, to
which we have affixed our Seals and figned our
Names. We now petition that you will be
pleafed to forward it : One Paper is the Original,
with our Seals and Signatures affixed, the other
a Copy under the Seal of the Cauzy, which you
will be pleafed to tranfmit to the Governor
General in Council of Calcutta, and requeft his

R

Lord-

Lordſhip will order it to be tranſlated, and ſend the Tranſlation with the Original to the Court of Directors.

A true Tranſlation.

(Signed)   G. F. CHERRY,
A true Copy.   D. P. T',
E. Hay,
Secʸ to the Fort.

t t.

Under the Seals and Signatures as under written.

We the Zemindars, Chowdries, and Talookdars, of the Mhals of Zellah Moorſhedabad, in Soubah of Bengal, have heard that the Gentlemen in England are diſpleaſed with Mr. Haſtings, on Suſpicion that he oppreſſed us Inhabitants of this Place, took our Money by Deceit and Force, and ruined the Country;— Therefore we, upon the Strength of our Religion and religious Tenets, which we hold as a Duty upon us, and in order to act conformable to the Decrees of God, in delivering Evidence, relate the praiſe-worthy Actions, full of Prudence and Rectitude, Friendſhip and Politeneſs, of Mr. Haſtings, poſſeſſed of great Abilities and Underſtanding; and by repreſenting Facts, remove the Doubts that have poſſeſſed the Minds of the Gentlemen in England: That Mr. Haſtings diſtributed Protection and Security to Religion, and Kindneſs and Peace to us all.   He is free from the Charge of Embezzlements and Fraud, and his Heart is void of

Covetouſ

Covetoufnefs and Avidity. During the Period
of his Government no one experienced from him
other than Protection and Juftice, never having
felt Hardfhips from him ; nor did the Poor ever
know the Weight of an oppreffive Hand from
him. Our Characters and Reputations have
been always guarded in Quiet from Attack by
the Vigilance of his Prudence and Forefight,
and preferved by the Terror of his Juftice. He
never omitted the fmalleft Inftance of Kindnefs
and Goodnefs towards us, and thofe entitled to
it ; but always applied, by Soothings and Mildnefs, the Salve of Comfort to the Wounds of
Affliction, not allowing a fingle Perfon to be
overpowered by Defpair. He difplayed his
Friendfhip and Kindnefs to all; he deftroyed
the Powers of Enemies and wicked Men by the
Strength of his Terror; he tied the Hands of
Tyrants and Oppreffors by his Juftice ; and by
this Conduct he fecured Happinefs and Joy to
us. He re-eftablifhed the Foundation of Juftice;
and we at all Times, during his Government,
lived in Comfort, and paffed our Days in Peace.
We are many, many of us fatisfied and pleafed
with him. As Mr. Haftings was perfectly well
acquainted with the Manners and Cuftoms of
thefe Countries, he was always defirous of performing that which would tend to the Prefervation of our Religion, and of the Duties of our
Sects, and guarded the religious Cuftoms of
each from the Effects of Misfortunes and Accidents. In every Senfe he treated us with Attention and Refpect.—We have reprefented
without Deceit what we have ourfelves feen,
and the Facts that happened from him.

The Seals and Signatures to this Addrefs, 94

The Four following in the fame Terms as the
laft.

Tranflation of a Perfian Addrefs from th
Canongoes of Jellafore, prefented by
their Vakeel.

U U.

*Paper delivered by the Vakeel from the Canoongoes,
Zemindars, Chowdries, and Talookdars, of
Chucklab Jelafore.*

The Seals and Signatures to this Addrefs,   19

Tranflation of a Perfian Addrefs from the
Zemindars of Dacca Jelalpore, prefented
by their Vakeel.

*Paper delivered by the Vakeel on the Part of the
Zemindars, Chowdries, and Talookdars, of the
Mbals of Pergunnah Jellalpore, &c. in the
Diftrict of Dacca.*

The Seals and Signatures to this Addrefs,   106

Tranflation of a Perfian Addrefs from the
Zemindars, &c. of Dacca Momun
Sing, prefented by their Vakeel.

W. W.

*Paper delivered by the Vakeel on the Part of the
Zemindars, Chowdries, and Talookdars of the
Mbals of Zillah Momenfing, &c. in the Diftrict
of Dacca.*

The Seals and Signatures to this Addrefs,   146

X X.

Tranflation of a Perfian Addrefs from the Zemindar of Beerbhoom, prefented by his Vakeel.

Papers delivered by Golaum Hyder Khan, Vakeel to the Zemindar of Purgunnab Beerbhoom, &c.

Petition under the Signature of Golaum, Hyder Khan, Vakeel to the Zemindar of Purgunnah Bheerbhoom.

MY Conftituent has prepared and written under his own Seal, and that of his principal Servants and Officers, an Addrefs relative to Mr. Haftings, which he has tranfmitted with a Copy to your Lordfhip, in the Hope that your Lordfhip will be pleafed to direct that it may be tranflated into Englifh, and the Original and Tranflation be forwarded to Europe.

The Seals and Signatures to this Addrefs, 14

A true Tranflation.
(Signed)   G. F. CHERRY,
D. P. T'.

A true Copy.
E. Hay,
Sec' to the Gov'.

13

Tranflation of a Perfian Addrefs from Khan Jehan Khan, and the reft of the Inhabitants of Hoogly, prefented by his Vakeel.

y y.

Papers delivered by Mahomed Mhyul Dien Khan, Vakeel to Khan Jehan Khan Behadre Jeffarut Jung.

Petition under the Signature of Mahomed Mhy Ul Dien Khan, Vakeel to Khan Jehan Khan Behadre Jeffarut Jung.

THE Refidents and Natives of the Bunder (Factory) of Houghly have written and affixed their Seals to an Addrefs relative to Mr. Haftings, and have tranfmitted the Original and Copy to your Lordfhip; I humbly requeft your Lordfhip will be pleafed to order the Addrefs to be tranflated by the public Officer of Government, and that the Tranflation and Original may be fent to Europe.

A true Tranflation.
(Signed)   G. F. CHERRY,
D. P. T.

A true Copy.
E. Hay,
Sec' to the Gov'.

y y.

We, the Inhabitants and Natives of the Bunder (Factory) of Houghly and its Environs, in the Soubah of Bengal, humbly reprefent to His Moft Gracious Majefty the King of England, and to the upright Affembly, the Comptrollers and Directors of the Company, that Mr. Haftings, from his Nomination to the Government of this Country until the Time of his Return to Europe, fecured our Satisfaction and Happinefs by his pleafing Deportment and commendable Virtues; he preferved the Affairs of this Country of every Denomination in the Channel of eftablifhed Ufage and Cuftom, fo that Mankind, whether Merchants, Officers, Travellers, Strangers, or Tradefmen, with the moft perfect Eafe of Mind and Security employed themfelves in feeking their Subfiftence, in Happinefs and inward Gratitude praying for the Extent of His Majefty's Reign, and the Company's Authority. That Gentleman was fo attentive to the Protection and Safety of the Country, that no Difturber or Rioter on any Side could extend the Hand of Oppreffion and Tyranny.—He eftablifhed Courts of Juftice according to the refpective Religions and Sects; and notwithftanding the Want of Rain, the dreadful Effects of Famine were warded off by the Wifdom and Prudence of his Meafures and Arrangements. He fettled the Courts of Criminal

minal and Civil Jurisdiction (Fouzedary and Dewany) on a new Footing, by which Mankind were guarded against Thieves and Murderers. He founded a College for the Propagation of Learning, and fixed an Income and Degrees for the Students, so that to this Moment the Learned and Students enjoy the Benefits and Advantages thereof, and pray for the Prosperity of His Majesty's Reign, and the Company; and we Moguls and others, whether Men in Service or Merchants, always lived protected from the Frauds of the Times under the Shadow of his Care and Kindness. He never coveted our Character, Property, or Wealth, nor did he ever act by Force or Opposition. In short, we, during the Government of Mr. Hastings, enjoyed Peace and Quiet, and in no Respect experienced Distress or Hardship, and are pleased with his Qualities and Virtues.

Written 11 Shabaan 1202 Hejeree,
17th May 1788.

The Seals to this Address, 43

Translation of a Persian Addrels from the Zemindar of Pachete, prefented by his Vakeel.

Z Z.

Papers delivered by the Vakeel of Maba Rajah Ragonaut Narain, Zemindar of Pachete.

Petition under the Seal and Name of Rajah Ragonaut Narain.

I HAVE prepared an Addrels under my Seal relative to Mr. Haftings, and tranfmit it to your Lordfhip, who, I hope, will be pleafed to order it to be publicly tranflated, and the Original and Tranflation be forwarded to Europe.

A true Tranflation.
(Signed) G. F. CHERRY,
D. P. T'.

A true Copy.
E. Hay,
Sec' to the Gov'.

Z Z.

Under the Seals and Signatures as under written.

I Ragonaut Narain, Zemindar of Pachete, in the Soubah of Bengal, have heard that the Gentlemen in England are difpleafed with Mr. Haftings on Sufpicion that he oppreffed us, Inhabitants of this Place, took our Money by

S Deceit

Deceit and Force, and ruined the Country ;—
Therefore we, upon the Strength of our Religion and religious Tenets, which we hold as a
Duty upon us; and in order to act conformable
to the Decrees of God in delivering Evidence,
relate the praise-worthy Actions, full of Prudence
and Rectitude, Friendship and Politeness, of
Mr. Haftings, poffeffed of great Abilities and
Underftanding ; and by reprefenting Facts, remove the Doubts that have poffeffed the Minds
of the Gentlemen in England : That Mr.
Haftings diftributed Protection and Security to
Religion, and Kindnefs and Peace to us all. He
is free from the Charge of Embezzlements and
Fraud, and his Heart is void of Covetoufnefs
and Avidity. During the Period of his Government no one experienced from him other than
Protection and Juftice, never having felt Hardfhips from him; nor did the Poor ever know
the Weight of an oppreffive Hand from him.
Our Character and Reputations have been always guarded in Quiet from Attack by the Vigilance of his Prudence and Forefight, and
preferved by the Terror of his Juftice. He
never omitted the fmalleft Inftance of Kindnefs
and Goodnefs towards us and thofe entitled to
it; but always applied, by Soothings and Mildnefs, the Salve of Comfort to the Wounds of
Affliction; not allowing a fingle Perfon to be
overpowered by Defpair. He difplayed his
Friendfhip and Kindnefs to all; he deftroyed
the Powers of Enemies and wicked Men by the
Strength of his Terror; he tied the Hands of
Tyrants and Oppreffors by his Juftice, and by
this Conduct he fecured Happinefs and Joy to
us. He re-eftablifhed the Foundation of Juftice;
and

and we at all Times during his Government
lived in Comfort, and paſſed our Days in Peace.
We are many, many of us ſatisfied and pleaſed
with him. As Mr. Haſtings was perfectly well
acquainted with the Manners, and Cuſtoms of
theſe Countries, he was always deſirous of performing that which would tend to the Preſervation of our Religion, and of the Duties of our
Sects; and guarded the religious Cuſtoms of
each from the Effects of Misfortunes and Accidents. In every Senſe he treated us with Attention and Reſpect.—We have repreſented
without Deceit what ourſelves have ſeen, and
the Facts that happened from him.

The Seals and Signatures to this Addreſs.

Maha Rajah Ragonaut Narain.
Kiſhen Caunt del Serma.
Colly Churn Serma.
Khoſaul Chund Serma.
Narain Serma.

A true Tranſlation.
(Signed) G. F. CHERRY,
D. P. T'.

A true Copy.
E. Hay,
Secr' to the Gov'.

S 2

Tranflation of a Perfian Addrefs from fome of the Inhabitants of Calcutta, which was delivered to the Secretary by Meer Zahed and others.

Tranflation of Petition delivered to Edward Hay, Efquire, Secretary to the Government, by Meer Zabid Mowlarry Abdoolah Moazim Ally and others, and Seyed Rook Ullah, the Vakeel of Meer Bendeh Ally Khan Behadre.

WE, the Inhabitants of the Town of Calcutta, having prepared an Addrefs relative to Mr. Haftings, under our Seals and Signatures, do prefent the fame, together with a Copy thereof, to the Council, having in their Kindnefs caufed this Addrefs to be tranflated by the Officers of the Company, will be pleafed to fend both the Original and the Tranflation to England.—We have thus requefted what was proper.

A true Tranflation.
(Signed) G. F. CHERRY,
D. P. T'.

A true Copy.
E. Hay,
Sec'y to the Gov'.

Tranſlation of the Addreſs delivered to Edward Hay, Eſq Secretary to the Government, by Meer Zabid, and other Inhabitants of Calcutta.

We, the great and principal People, Merchants, and others, Men of different Sects and Perſuaſions, Inhabitants of the City of Calcutta, Part of the Territories of the Engliſh Company (whom may God long preſerve in Proſperity) having heard that the exalted Rulers of England, and they who preſide over the Courts of Juſtice, have received Diſpleaſure in their humane Hearts againſt Mr. Haſtings, upon Suſpicion that he took the Money and Effects of us the Inhabitants of this Country by Fraud and Treachery, and entirely ruined the Government of the Company:—Therefore we, the People aforeſaid, with a perfect Unanimity, both in Expreſſion and Meaning, according to the Precepts of our ſeveral Religions and Cuſtoms, the Obſervance of which we always make the Object of our Hearts, do, for the Purpoſe of diſpelling the Doubts of the exalted Gentlemen aforeſaid, bring from behind the Curtain of Concealment, and place upon the public Seat of Notoriety, ſuch a Repreſentation of the Character, and ſuch a Relation of the Words and Actions of Mr. Haſtings, whoſe Diſpoſition is worthy of all Praiſe, as is true and certain, and fully proved and clearly demonſtrated, and free from Ornament and Exaggeration. From the Time that he was appointed to, and became inveſted with, the Government of Calcutta, till the End of his Adminiſtration, he was always occupied in the Welfare of the Reyats, and the Improvement
of

of the Country, in the Support of the Weak,
in healing the Oppreffions and Injuftice of bad
Men, in good Offices to the great and fmall,
in the Prefervation of the Rules of Government, and in Attention to the Rights and Degrees of Men nobly defcended, in the Encouragement of Men of Merit and Learning, in
laying the Foundations of Virtue, as for Example, by building Colleges and Schools, in
keeping alive the Learning of every Sect and
Perfuafion, In giving Eafe to the Landholders
and the Merchants, in difpenfing Juftice to the
injured and oppreffed, in fpeaking the Language
of Confolation to the humble as well as to the
great, in conciliating the Hearts of Princes,
whether Friends or Enemies, and in the Welfare of the Company.—In fhort, throughout
the Territories under the Government of the
Company there is not a fingle Individual who
has not received from the well-fpread Table of
Mr. Haftings's Bounty whatever he was entitled
to ; and we, the Inhabitants of this Town of Calcutta, have for our Parts reprefented only that
which we have ourfelves feen of the Kindnefs,
the Care, the Knowledge of what was right,
and the Humanity of Mr. Haftings, who could
diftinguifh what was juft from what was unjuft,
who in his Exemption from Avarice was unequalled, the Fountain of good Difpofitions,
and the Affemblage of Mercies; we were and
are in every Way fatisfied with and grateful to
Mr. Haftings, and fweet and refrefhing to our
Tongues are the Words with which we utter his
Praifes.

Written on 2d of Bhaudan,
16th Aug. 1788.
The Seals and Signature to this Addrefs, 448
9

Copy Tranſlation of a Perſian Addreſs from
other Inhabitants of the Town of Calcutta; which was delivered to the Secretary by Rupie Loll Dutt, and others.

C C.

*Tranſlation of a Petition from Ruſſick Loll Dutt,
and Nemoy Churn Mullick, and Govind Chund
Byſauk, and Loll Chund Mittre, and Nilly
Anund Sein, and others, delivered by them to Edward Hay, Eſq. Secretary to the Government.*

WE, your Petitioners, Inhabitants of the
Town of Calcutta, do preſent to the
Council an Addreſs, which we have prepared
under Signatures, relative to the Buſineſs of Mr.
Haſtings, together with a Copy thereof; and
we do requeſt, in behalf of ourſelves and other
Perſons who have ſigned the ſaid Addreſs, that
the Council, having in their Kindneſs cauſed the
ſame to be tranſlated by the Officers of the
Company, will be pleaſed to forward the Original and the Tranſlation to England: What was
neceſſary we have ſtated.—Furthermore, may
the Sun of your Life and Proſperity ever remain
reſplendent.

A true Tranſlation.
(Signed) G. F. CHERRY.
D. P. T.

Translation of the Address delivered to Edward
Hay, Esq. Secretary to the Government, by
Ruffick Loll Dutt, Nemoy Churn Mullick,
and others, Inhabitants of Calcutta.

It having at this Time come to the Hearing
of all us the Gentry, Merchants, and other
principal People of the City of Calcutta, Part
of the Territories of the brave and noble English Company, (whom may God long preserve in
Prosperity!) that the exalted Rulers of England, and they who preside over the Courts of
Justice, have received Doubt and Displeasure in
their just Hearts against Mr. Hastings, upon a
Suspicion that, taking the Money and Effects of
us the Inhabitants of this Country by various
Frauds and Artifices, he ruined the Government of the Company;—Therefore we, the
People aforesaid, with a perfect Unanimity both
in Expression and Meaning, do from our Hearts,
and according to what we know and have
heard, lay before the exalted Gentlemen aforesaid, for the Purpose of dispelling their Doubts,
a true Representation of the Character of Mr.
Hastings, from the Time that he was appointed
to, and became invested with, the Government
of Calcutta till the End of his Administration.
He was always occupied in the Welfare of the
Ryotts and the Improvement of the Country, in
the Support of the Weak, in healing the Op-
pressions and Injustice of bad Men, good
Offices to the Great and Small, in the Preservation of the Rules of Government, and
in Attention to the Rights and Degrees of
Men nobly descended, in the Encouragement

ment of Men of Merit and Learning, in esta-
blishing Allowances for Mussulmen, Doctors,
and for Pundits and Students, and in support-
ing Colleges and Schools both for Mussulmans
and Hindoos, in keeping alive the Learning
of every Sect and Persuasion, in giving Ease to
the Landholders and the Merchants, in dis-
pensing Justice to the injured and oppressed, in
speaking the Language of Consolation to the
Humble as well as the Great, in conciliating
the Hearts of Princes, whether Friends or Enemies, and in the Welfare of the Company. In
short, throughout the Territories under the Government of the Company, there is not a single
Individual who has not received from the Table
of Mr. Hastings's Bounty whatever he was entitled to: And we, the Inhabitants of this
Town of Calcutta, have for our own Parts represented only that which we have ourselves seen
and heard of the Kindness, the Care, the
Knowledge of what was right, and the Humanity of Mr. Hastings, who could distinguish
what was just from what was unjust, who, in
his Exemption from Avarice, was unequalled,
the Fountain of good Dispositions, and the As-
semblage of Mercies. We were and are satisfied with and grateful to Mr. Hastings; and
sweet and refreshing to our Tongues are the
Words with which we utter his Praises. Written the 7th of Assin, 21st September 1788.
The Seals and Signatures to this Address, 160.

A true Translation.

G. F. CHERRY,
D. P. T.

A true Copy.

E. Hay,
Secr^y to the Gov^t.

T

Translation of a Persian Address from other Inhabitants of the Town of Calcutta, which was delivered to the Secretary by Rauje Chund Roy, and others.

Translation of a Petition delivered to Edward Hay, Esquire, the Secretary of the Government, by Rauje Chund Roy, Pettumber Mittre, Durup Narain, Colly Perfaud Ghofe, Tunnoor Dutt, and others, Inhabitants of the Town of Calcutta.

WE, your Petitioners, Inhabitants of the Town of Calcutta, prefent to the Council an Addrefs relative to Mr. Haftings, under our Seals and Signatures, together with a Copy thereof; and in behalf of ourfelves, and of the other Perfons who have fealed or figned the faid Addrefs, do requeft, that the Council, having caufed the fame to be tranflated by the Officers of the Company, will be pleafed to tranfmit the Original and the Tranflation to England.

What was neceffary we have reprefented.

Translation of the Address delivered to Edward Hay, Esquire, Secretary to the Government, by Rauje Chund Roy, Pettumber Mittre, and others.

We, the greateft and principal People, Merchants, and others, Men of different Sects and Perfuafions, Inhabitants of the City of Calcutta, Part of the Territories of the Englifh Company, (whom may God long preferve in Profperity!)

Profperity!) having heard that the exalted
Rulers of England, and they who preside over
the Courts of Juftice, have received Difpleafure
in their humane Hearts againft Mr. Haftings,
upon a Sufpicion that he took the Money and
Effects of us the Inhabitants of this Country by
Fraud and Treachery, and entirely ruined the
Government of the Company;—Therefore we,
the People aforefaid, with a perfect Unanimity
both in Expreffion and Meaning, according to
the Precepts of our feveral Religions and Cuftoms, the Obfervance of which we always make
the Objects of our Hearts, do, for the Purpofe
of difpelling the Doubts of the exalted Gentlemen aforefaid, bring from behind the Curtain
of Concealment, and place upon the public Seat
of Notoriety, fuch a Reprefentation of the Character, and fuch a Relation of the Words and
Actions of Mr. Haftings, whofe Difpofition is
worthy of all Praife, as is true, and certain, and
fully proved, and clearly demonftrated, and free
from Ornament and Exaggeration, from the
Time that he was appointed to and became
invefted with the Government of Calcutta, till
the End of the Adminiftration.—He was always
occupied in the Welfare of the Reyats, and the
Improvement of the Country; in the Support of
the Weak, in healing the Oppreffions and Injuftice of bad Men, in good Offices to the Great
and Small, in the Prefervation of the Rules of
Government, and in Attention to the Right
and Degrees of Men nobly defcended, in the
Encouragement of Men of Merit and Learning, in laying the Foundations of Virtue, as for
Example, by building Colleges and Schools, in
keeping alive the Learning of every Sect and

Perfuafion,

(148)

Perſuaſion, in giving Eaſe to the Landholders and the Merchants, in diſpenſing Juſtice to the Afflicted and Oppreſſed, in ſpeaking the Language of Conſolation to the Humble as well as to the Great, in conciliating the Hearts of Princes, whether Friends or Enemies, and in the Welfare of the Company; in ſhort, throughout the Territories under the Government of the Company, there is not a ſingle Individual who has not received from the well-ſpread Table of Mr. Haſtings's Bounty whatever he was entitled to.—And we, the Inhabitants of this Town of Calcutta, have for our own Part repreſented, only that which we have ourſelves ſeen of the Kindneſs, the Care, the Knowledge of what was right, and the Humanity of Mr. Haſtings, who could diſtinguiſh what was juſt from what was unjuſt, who, in his Exemption from Avarice, was unequalled; the Fountain of good Diſpoſitions, and the Aſſemblage of Mercies.—We were and are in every Way ſatisfied with and grateful to Mr. Haſtings; and ſweet and refreſhing to our Tongues are the Words with which we utter his Praiſes.——Written on the 2d Bhaudun, 16th Auguſt 1788.

The Seals and Signatures to this Addreſs, 518.

A true Tranſlation.
(Signed) G. F. CHERRY,
D. P. Tʳ.

A true Copy.
E. Hay,
Secrʸ to the Govᵗ.

Letter

Letter from the Rector and Churchwarden of the Greek Church.

To Edward Hay, Esq. Secretary to the Government.

Sir,

ENCLOSED we have the Honour to send you an Addrefs to the Court of Directors in favour of Mr. Haftings, figned by ourfelves and all other the principal Members of the Greek Church in Bengal. The original Addrefs in modern Greek is accompanied by a Copy and an English Tranflation of it. The Original and the Tranflation, we humbly requeft, may be tranfmitted to the Honourable Court of Directors by the earlieft Conveyance.

We have the Honour to be,

Sir,

Fort William,   Your moft obedient
8 January 1789.   humble Servants,

(Signed) C. PORRTHENIO, Rector
of the Greek Church of Calcutta.

(Signed) MAUNODY KYRIAKOR,
Churchwarden.

A true Copy.

E. Hay,

Sec[y] to the Gov[t].

Copy

Copy Translation of a Greek Address from the Rector, and other Members, of the Greek Church.

Translation of an Address from the principal Members of the Greek Church in Bengal, to the Honourable Court of Directors of the East India Company.

WE the Offspring of Hellass, called by Europeans Greeks, now residing for commercial Purposes in Calcutta, and other Places in the Kingdom of Bengal, all and each of whom, except only One or Two, came into this Country since the Commencement of the Administration of Warren Hastings, the late glorious and exalted Governor of Bengal, and of all East India, trading in and about these Parts free and unmolested.—We, the said Greeks, during the happy Days of the said late Governor Warren Hastings, having often been protected, and justly supported, by him, and having also been encouraged by his noble Succour and Assistance to raise, in this City, a holy Temple, in Honour and Glory of our Saviour's Transfiguration in Mount Thabor, to the End that we might be fixed in this Country, and that this our Church should remain as the Foundation of an Establishment for us, and for our Successors, being of the same Nation and Religion: We, at the same Time, considering ourselves lawful Subjects of his most high, powerful, and sacred Majesty the King of Great Britain, for whose Permanence, Prosperity, and Happiness,

Happiness, we, as by our Duty indispensably
bound, do offer up to the Almighty God our
daily Prayers: For as much as we have heard,
with deep Regret, that the said late Governor
General Warren Haftings is profecuted, and
being, on our Parts, moft perfectly and heartily
fatisfied with his wife and upright Government,
as well as gratified by the pious and great Works
which he rendered to us with his ufual Benevolence—do take the Liberty of teftifying and declaring, by this humble Reprefentation, his
Chriftian and univerfal Character, his Beneficence and charitable Difpofition towards all
Mankind, his juft and impartial Love for all
the Native Inhabitants, whether high or low, of
this Kingdom, and his fervent Zeal for the
Profperity of the Country in general, and of
every Individual, manifefting to all and every
of them Marks of paternal Affection, and
ftretching forth his Hand to thofe whom he
found in indigent Circumftances, and deftitute
of the Neceffaries of Life. He was a zealous
Patron for the Difpenfation of Juftice to every
Individual, and a faithful Balance of Equity. In
a Word, he was enriched with all humane and
moral Endowments, and famous not only for
his moral and political Virtues, but worthy of
Praife, and to be highly fpoken of for his Defire
to obtain and to improve the Literature of this
Country. All which Excellencies will render
him admired, and immortal, throughout the
univerfal World.

We therefore, the fmall Number of Greeks
refiding in Calcutta, and difperfed throughout
Bengal, in true Teftimony of our great Gratitude for the many Benefits which we have received from the late Governor, Warren Haf-

7 . tings,

tings, do join with all the World in declaring
our Sentiments, in favour of the Character of
our worthy, wife, and humane Patron, the late
Governor General; and have hereunto humbly
fet our Hands, this 13th Day of December
1788, O. S.

Parthenio, Rector of the Church of Calcutta,
and a Native of Corfew.

Nathaniel, a Native of Cyphanus, a Prieſt
and Monk of the Convent of Mount Sinai,
and Rector of the Church at Calcutta.

Panageotes Alexius, of Philiopolis.

Mavrodis Hiriacos, Warden of the Church at
Calcutta, and a Native of Phyliopolis.

George Leondew, a Native of Smyrna.

Demetrius Georgius, from Bythenia.

Shereen Hadjy, Ibraheem of Cæſaria.

Athenaſias Theodore, from Pruſa.

Theo Charis, from Arta.

Joannes Demetrius, from Mytilyne.

Jacobus Haujy Hoſma, from Cæſaria.

Angelus Dadelco, from Philiopolis.

Chriſtodolo, Son of Papa Nicolai, from the
Iſland of Neos.

Panageotis Demetrius, from Kely.

Angelos Doocos, of the Iſland of Corfew.

Chriſtodolos Mavrody, of Philiopolis.

Emanuel Demetrius, of Albania.

Demetrius Galonos, from Athens.

Georgius Panageotis, from Phyliopolis.

Alexandros Panageotis, from Dº.

Anaſtaſius Dº, from Dº.

Joannes Dº, from Dº.

Potos Haujy Abraham, from Cæſaria.

Jacob Dº Iſaah, from Dº.

Alexius

Alexius Haujy Abraham, from Cæfaria.
Simeon D⁰ ᵈ ᴵᶜ D⁰, ᵍ ᶦffrom D⁰.
Joſeph D⁰. ᵒⁿᵘ D⁰ ᵇʳfrom D⁰.
Johannes D⁰ Maᵗⁿ, ᵘ from D⁰.
Lucos Theodore, from Magnefia.
George Careeda, from Phyliopolis.
Soures Anthony, from D⁰.
George Athenafius, from D⁰.
Conftantinus Theodorus, from D⁰.
    D⁰ Shahing, from D⁰.
Michael Andrew, from D⁰.
Demetrius George Calogrethy, from the
    Ifland of Neos.
George Demetrius, from D⁰.
Nicholas Marinus Calonas, from D⁰
Marinus Nicholas Calonas, from D⁰.
Demetrius Chriftodolo, from Phylopopolis.
Michael, from Conftantinople.
George Alexander, from Phylopopolis.
Leontheus Chriftodolo, from D⁰.
Alexander Keeriacos, from D⁰.
Bafileus Haujy Contrantine, from D⁰.
Simeon Georgia, from Georgia.
Michael Anthony, from the Ifland of
    Naxia.
George Anthony, Native of Calcutta.
Theodorus James, from the Ifland of
    Samos.
Nicholas, from Crete.
Sabas, a Sclavonian.
Pannagiotis, from Kheletos.
George Angelo, from Phylopopolis.
Conftantine of Trapazandios.
Jordan, from Cæfaria.
Joannes Garaganos, from Georgia.
Anaftafius Conftantine, from Phylopopolis.
U   Soteres

Soteres Slogew, from Phyliopopolis.
Nicholas Spiredon, from Crete.
George, from Aphalonia.
Stamatis Demetrius, from Rhodes.
Zacharius, from D°.
John, from Kely.
Athanafios Demetrius, from Phylopopolis.
Demetrius Eleijah, from D°.
George Angala, from D°.
Anthony Phofkolos, from the Ifland of
    Jineus.
Mathew Anthony, from D°.
Joannes, from Khely.
Thalifinos Haujy Peter, from Trapezon.
Boikos Neno, from Phylopopolis.
Paulee Stratee, from Myteline.

A true Tranflation.

(Signed) C. PARTHENIO.

A true Copy.

    E. Hay,
    Sec' to the Gov'.

Tranflation of Perfian Addreffes from the
Rajah of Tumlook; from the Ranny of
Myfadel; from the Ranny of Hidgelee;
from the Rajah of Hidgelee; and from
the Rajah of Sujamootah; prefented by
their Vakeels.

k k.

*Paper delivered by the Vakeel on the Part of Rajah
Anundenarain, Zemindar of Pergunnah Tumlook
17 Anna Share, and tranflated purfuant to an
Order from the Governor General in Council,
dated 27th April 1788.*

Under the Seal of Rajah Anundernarain, Zemindar of Purgunnah Tumlook (7 Anna
Share).

I Have heard that the Gentlemen in England
are difpleafed with Mr. Haftings, on Sufpicion that he oppreffed us Inhabitants of this
Place, took our Money by Deceit and Force,
and ruined the Country; therefore we, upon
the Strength of our Religion and religious Tenets, which we hold as a Duty upon us, and in
order to act conformable to the Decrees of God
in delivering Evidence, relate the praife-worthy
Actions, full of Prudence and Rectitude, Friendfhip and Politenefs, of Mr. Haftings, poffeffed
of great Abilities and Underftanding; and by
reprefenting Facts, remove the Doubts that
have poffeffed the Minds of the Gentlemen in
England; that Mr. Haftings diftributed Protection and Security to Religion, and Kindnefs

and

and Peace to us all. He is free from the
Charge of Embezzlements and Fraud, and his
Heart is void of Covetousness and Avidity.
During the Period of his Government, no one
experienced from him other than Protection
and Justice, never having felt Hardships from
him, nor did the Poor ever know the Weight of
an oppressive Hand from him; our Characters
and Reputations have been always guarded in
Quiet from Attack by the Vigilance of his Prudence and Foresight, and preserved by the
Terror of his Justice; he never omitted the
smallest Instance of Kindness and Goodness
towards us and those entitled to it, but always
applied, by Soothings and Mildness, the Salve
of Comfort to the Wounds of Affliction, not
allowing a single Person to be overpowered by
Despair; he displayed his Friendship and Kindness to all; he destroyed the Powers of Enemies
and wicked Men by the Strength of his Terror;
he tied the Hands of Tyrants and Oppressors by
his Justice, and by this Conduct he secured Happiness and Joy to us; he re-established the Foundation of Justice, and we at all Times, during
his Government, lived in Comfort, and passed
our Days in Peace. We are many, many of us
satisfied and pleased with him. As Mr. Hastings was perfectly well acquainted with the
Manners and Customs of these Countries, he was
always desirous of performing that which would
tend to the Preservation of our Religion, and of
the Duties of our Sects, and guarded the religious Customs of each from the Effects of Misfortunes and Accidents. In every Sense he
treated us with Attention and Respect.—We
have

have reprefented without Deceit what we have ourfelves feen, and the Facts that happened from him.

A true Tranflation.
(Signed)   G. F. CHERRY,
D. P. T'.

A true Copy.
E. Hay,
Sec.y to the Govern.t.

11.

Paper delivered by the Vakeel on the Part of the Ranny Jannekee, Zemindar of Purgunnab Myfaudul, &c. and tranflated purfuant to an Order from the Governor General in Council, dated 27th April 1788.

Under the Seal of Ranny Jannekee, Zemindar of Purgunnah Myfaudel.

I have heard that the Gentlemen in England are difpleafed with Mr. Haftings, on Sufpicion that he oppreffed us Inhabitants of this Place, took our Money by Deceit and Force, and ruined the Country;—Therefore we, upon the Strength of our Religion and religious Tenets, which we hold as a Duty upon us, and in order to act conformably to the Decrees of God in delivering Evidence, relate the praife-worthy Actions, full of Prudence and Rectitude, Friendfhip and Politenefs, of Mr. Haftings, poffeffed of great Abilities and Underftanding; and by reprefenting Facts, remove the Doubts that have poffeffed the Minds of the Gentlemen in England; that Mr. Haftings diftributed Protection and Security to Religion, and Kindnefs
and

and Peace to us all. He is free from the Charge
of Embezzlements and Fraud, and his Heart is
void of Covetoufnefs and Avidity. During the
Period of his Government, no one experienced
from him other than Protection and Juftice,
never having felt Hardfhips from him; nor did
the Poor ever know the Weight of an oppreffive
Hand from him. Our Characters and Reputations have been always guarded in Quiet from
Attack, by the Vigilance of his Prudence and
Forefight, and preferved by the Terror of his
Juftice. He never omitted the fmalleft Inftance
of Kindnefs and Goodnefs towards us, and thofe
entitled to it; but always applied, by Soothings
and Mildnefs, the Salve of Comfort to the
Wounds of Affliction, not allowing a fingle
Perfon to be overpowered by Defpair. He difplayed his Friendfhip and Kindnefs to all; he
deftroyed the Powers of Enemies and wicked
Men by the Strength of his Terror; he tied the
Hands of Tyrants and Oppreffors by his Juftice;
and by this Conduct he fecured Happinefs and
Joy to us. He re-eftablifhed the Foundation
of Juftice; and we at all Times, during his Government, lived in Comfort, and paffed our
Days in Peace. We are many, many of us
fatisfied and pleafed with him. As Mr. Haftings
was perfectly well acquainted with the Manners
and Cuftoms of thefe Countries, he was always
defirous of performing that which would tend to
the Prefervation of our Religion, and of the
Duties of our Sects, and guarded the religious
Cuftoms of each from the Effects of Misfortunes
and Accidents. In every Senfe he treated us
with Attention and Refpect.—We have reprefented without Deceit what we have ourfeives
feen, and the Facts that happened from him.

. m m.

*Paper delivered by the Vakeel on the Part of the
Ranny Sougundah, Zemindah of Dooroodumnam
and Manchamootah, &c. in Chucla Hidglee,
and translated pursuant to an Order from the
Governor General in Council, dated 27th April
1788.*

Under the Seal of Ranny Sougundah, Zemindar
of Dooroodumnam and Manchamootah, &c.
in Chucla Hidgelee.

I have heard that the Gentlemen in England
are displeased with Mr. Haftings, on Sufpicion
that he oppreffed us Inhabitants of this Place,
took our Money by Deceit and Force, and
ruined the Country——Therefore we, upon the
Strength of our Religion and religious Tenets,
which we hold as a Duty upon us, and in order
to act conformable to the Decrees of God in
delivering Evidence, relate the praife-worthy
Actions, full of Prudence and Rectitude, Friendfhip and Politeneſs, of Mr. Haftings, poffeffed
of great Abilities and Underftanding ; and by
reprefenting Facts, remove the Doubts that have
poffeffed the Minds of the Gentlemen in England; that Mr. Haftings diftributed Protection
and Security to Religion, and Kindneſs and
Peace to us all. He is free from the Charge of
Embezzlements and Fraud, and his Heart is
void of Covetoufneſs and Avidity. During the
Period of his Government, no one experienced
from him other than Protection and Juftice,
never having felt Hardfhips from him ; nor did
the Poor even know the Weight of an oppreffive
Hand from him. Our Characters and Reputa-

8   tions

tions have been always guarded in Quiet from Attack by the Vigilance of his Prudence and Foresight, and preserved by the Terror of his Justice. He never omitted the smallest Instance of Kindness and Goodness towards us, and those, entitled to it, but always applied, by Soothings and Mildness, the Salve of Comfort to the Wounds of Affliction, not allowing a single Person to be overpowered by Despair. He displayed his Friendship and Kindness to all. He destroyed the Powers of Enemies and wicked Men by the Strength of his Terror. He tied the Hands of Tyrants and Oppressors by his Justice; and, by this Conduct, he secured Happiness and Joy to us. He re-established the Foundation of Justice; and we, at all Times during his Government, lived in Comfort, and passed our Days in Peace. We are many, many of us satisfied and pleased with him. As Mr. Hastings was perfectly well acquainted with the Manners and Customs of these Countries, he was always desirous of performing that which would tend to the Preservation of our Religion and of the Duties of our Sects, and guarded the religious Customs of each from the Effects of Misfortunes and Accidents. In every Sense he treated us with Attention and Respect.—We have represented without Deceit what we have ourselves seen, and the Facts that happened from him.

A true Translation.

(Signed)· G. F. CHERRY,
D. P. T'.

A true Copy.

E. Hay,
Sec' to the Gov'.

n n.

Paper delivered by the Vakeel on the Part of Rajah Beernarain, of Pergunnah Jellamootah, &c. in Chucla Hidgelee, and translated pursuant to an Order from the Governor General in Council, dated 27th April 1788.

Under the Seal of Rajah Beernarain, Zemindar of Pergunnah Jellamoth, &c. in Chucla Hidgelee.

I have heard that the Gentlemen in Eng-land are displeased with Mr. Hastings, on Suspicion that he oppressed us, Inhabitants of this Place, took our Money by Deceit and Force, and ruined the Country; therefore we, upon the Strength of our Religion and religious Tenets, which we hold as a Duty upon us, and in order to act conformable to the Decrees of God in delivering Evidence, relate the praiseworthy Actions, full of Prudence and Rectitude, Friendship and Politeness, of Mr. Hastings, possessed of great Abilities and Understanding; and by representing Facts remove the Doubts that have possessed the Minds of the Gentlemen in England; that 'Mr. Hastings distributed Protection and Security to Religion, and Kindness and Peace to us all; he is free from the Charge of Embezzlements and Fraud, and his Heart is void of Covetousness and Avidity. During the Period of his Government, no-one experienced from him other than Protection and Justice, never having felt Hardships from him. Our

X   Characters

Characters and Reputations have been always
guarded in Quiet from Attack, by the Vigilance of his Prudence and Foresight, and preserved by the Terror of his Justice. He never
omitted the smallest Instance of Kindness and
Goodness towards us, and those entitled to it;
but always applied, by Soothings and Mildness,
the Salve of Comfort to the Wounds of Affliction, not allowing a single Person to be overpowered by Despair. He displayed his Friendship and Kindness to all; he destroyed the
Powers of Enemies and wicked Men by the
Strength of his Terror; he tied the Hands of
Tyrants and Oppressors by his Justice; and by
this Conduct he secured Happiness and Joy to
us. He established the Foundation of Justice;
and we at all Times, during his Government,
lived in Comfort, and passed our Days in Peace.
We are many, many of us, satisfied and pleased
with him. As Mr. Hastings was perfectly
well acquainted with the Manners and Customs
of these Countries, he was always desirous of
performing that which would tend to the Preservation of our Religion, and of the Duties of
our Sects, and guarded the religious Customs of
each from the Effects of Misfortunes and Accidents. In every Sense he treated me with Attention and Respect.—We have represented
without Deceit what we have ourselves seen,
and the Facts that happened from him.

A true Translation.

G. F. CHERRY,
D. P. T.

A true Copy.

E. Hay,
Sec' to the Fort.

Comp'
Andr" Gardener.

O O.

Paper delivered by the Vakeel on the Part of Rajah Debindurnarain, Zemindar of Purgunnah Soujahmootah, and tranflated purfuant to an Order from the Governor General in Council, dated 27th April 1788.

Under the Seal of Rajah Debindurnarain, Zemindar of Purgunnah Soujahmootah.

I have heard that the Gentlemen in England are difpleafed with Mr. Haftings, on Sufpicion that he oppreffed us Inhabitants of this Place, took our Money by Deceit and Force, and ruined the Country :—Therefore we, upon the Strength of our Religion and religious Tenets, which we hold as a Duty upon us, and in order to act conformable to the Decrees of God in delivering Evidence, relate the praife-worthy Actions, full of Prudence and Rectitude, Friendfhip and Politenefs, of Mr. Haftings, poffeffed of great Abilities and Underftanding; and by reprefenting Facts, remove the Doubts that have poffeffed the Minds of the Gentlemen in England : That Mr. Haftings diftributed Protection and Security to Religion, and Kindnefs and Peace to us all. He is free from the Charge of Embezzlement and Fraud, and his Heart is void of Covetoufnefs and Avidity. During the Period of his Government, no one experienced from him other than Protection and Juftice, never having felt Hardfhips from him; nor did the Poor ever know the Weight of an oppreffive Hand from him. Our

Charac-

Characters and Reputations have been always
guarded in Quiet from Attack, by the Vigilance
of his Prudence and Foresight, and preserved by
the Terror of his Justice ; he never omitted the
smallest Instance of Kindness and Goodness towards us, and those entitled to it, but always
applied, by Soothings and Mildness, the Salve
of Comfort to the Wounds of Affliction, not
allowing a single Person to be overpowered by
Despair; he displayed his Friendship and Kindness to all; he destroyed the Powers of Enemies and wicked Men by the Strength of his
Terror; he tied the Hands of Tyrants and Oppressors by his Justice, and by this Conduct he
secured Happiness and Joy to us; he re-established the Foundation of Justice, and we at all
Times, during his Government, lived in Comfort, and passed our Days in Peace. We are
many, many of us satisfied and pleased with
him. As Mr. Hastings was perfectly well acquainted with the Manners and Customs of these
Countries, he was always desirous of performing that which would tend to the Preservation
of our Religion, and of the Duties of our
Sects, and guard the religious Customs of each
from the Effects of Misfortunes and Accidents.
In every Sense he treated us with Attention and
Respect.—We have represented without Deceit what we have ourselves seen, and the Facts
that happened from him.

A true Translation.
(Signed) G. F. CHERRY.
D. P. T^r.

A true Copy.
E. Hay,
Sect^y to the Fort.

CONCLUSION.

IN addition to the Teftimonials, which were
printed by Order of the Houfe of Commons;
the Nabob Fyzoola Cawn tranfmitted a Letter to the Court of Directors, in the Year
1786, through Mr. Haftings, expreffive of his
Attachment to the Company, and the Satisfaction which that Gentleman's Conduct had given
him. A very ftrong Teftimonial has alfo been
received from the Nabob of Arcot, by Mr.
Haftings; and another from Madajee Sindia,
both fully authenticated; but as they were not
tranfmitted directly to the Company, they could
not be laid upon the Table of the Houfe of
Commons. It may perhaps be deemed neceffary, to complete the Subject, to publifh
the Addreffes from the Britifh Inhabitants of
Calcutta, and the Officers of the Bengal Army.
They have already been publifhed both in India
and in England; but we reprint them, that the
whole Subject may appear in one Point of
View.

To the Honourable Warren Haftings Efquire,
Governor General.

SIR,

WE, the Britifh Inhabitants of Calcutta, im-
preffed with 1st Concern at your Departure from India, intreat your Acceptance of this
public Tribute, in Teftimony of our general
Satisfaction in the whole Tenour of your long
Adminiftration, and our lafting Senfe of your
many patriotic Exertions.

For a Series of Years, we have uninterrupt-
edly enjoyed, under your Government, the
Bleffings of private Comfort, and public Tranquillity, and no one can recollect a Period
wherein impartial Juftice, political Wifdom,
and a liberal Attention to the Rights of Individuals, were more eminently confpicuous.

We have feen you in many of the moft cri-
tical Situations to which political Life can be
expofed; in none of thefe have we perceived
you to deviate from the Dignity of your Station, the Integrity of your Character, or the
Vigour of your public Conduct: In every Vicif-
fitude you have been provident and collected,
and whilft you have proved yourfelf invulne-
rable to Infurrection, you have equally difplayed
yourfelf fuperior to Calumny.

The grand Outlines of the Connection by
which this Country is united to Great Britain
have

have been, under your Auspices, precisely ascertained, and its Continuance decisively secured. The unwieldy System of the double Government has been reduced to Order and Simplicity. The Administration of civil and criminal Justice, instead of a Burthen on Individuals, or an Engine of Corruption, has under your prudent Reformation become a Blessing to ten Millions of People. Arts have been uniformly patronised. The Channels of Communication between ourselves and the Natives have, by your liberal Encouragements, been opened, and our Settlement has increased to a Degree of Magnitude and Splendour, which evinces the Wisdom of your Measures, and the Mildness of your Government.

While the rest of India looked up to you alone for their Preservation from the Distractions of War and the Desolations of Famine, we have enjoyed an uninterrupted Plenty and Security, Blessings which, while we continue to possess, we shall never cease to remember were procured for us by your spirited Measures, which have raised upon the most solid Basis the Superstructure of public Happiness.

May that Happiness, and every other, be secured to you during the remaining Period of your Life, which can arise from the Possession of unsullied Virtue, and the Consciousness of unremitted Labours for the good of Society; and may you be blest, on your Return, with the brightest Reward a Patriot Mind can court, the Applause of your Sovereign, and the Gratitude

6   of

of a Country to which you have proved yourfelf fo illuftrious an Ornament.

We have the Honour to be,

Honourable Sir,

Your moft obedient,

Calcutta,   Humble Servants,

1ft Feb. 1785.   &c. &c.

Signed by 290 Perfons.

To Warren Haftings Efquire.

SIR,

SOON after your Departure from Bengal, it
was refolved, at a Meeting of Officers at the
Prefidency, that an Addrefs to you, as Governor General, fhould be figned, and forwarded
by the firft fafe Conveyance: And the Officers
were pleafed to make choice of us to fend forth
the Copies for Signatures, to receive them when
figned, and to fend them to you afterwards.

The Original confifts of eighteen Copies of
the fame Addrefs, which were fent in Duplicate
to the different military Stations; we received
all back except two Duplicates, and from the
complete Set two notorial Copies have been
made of the Addrefs and the Signatures of the
whole.

We have now the Honour to fend to you one
notorial Copy, together with a Copy of our
circular Letter.

We

We fhall, by the Ships of the Seafon, forward the other notorial Copy, and the Set of Originals of Sixteen, together with notorial Copies of the other two ; and we fhall lodge in the Hands of Colonel Pearfe the complete Set of Original, to be ready in cafe of Accidents to thefe, and ultimately to be forwarded to you, unlefs the Set of Originals firft fent fhould happily arrive ; in which cafe he will fend the two which now we deem it neceffary to keep by us, to prevent lofing the Means of conveying to you the Sentiments of our Brother Officers, if needful, hereafter.

We beg leave to affure you, that we receive the greateft Happinefs from having been chofen to be the Agents of fo refpectable a Body of Officers, and hope the Share we have had in promoting the Wifhes of our Friends and Conftituents will prove acceptable to you. We are,

With the higheft Refpect,

Sir,

Your moft obedient Servants,

T. D. PEARSE,
Colonel.

Calcutta,
5th Aug. 1785.

JAs MORGAN,
Colonel.

HENRY WATSON,
Lieut. Colonel, and
Chief Engineer.

Y

To the Honourable Warren Haftings, Efq. Governor General, &c.

SIR,

WE whofe Names are hereunto fubfcribed, Officers of the Bengal Army, with profound Refpect, and moft perfect Efteem, take the Liberty of addreffing you on your Departure from amongft us.

Many of us as Citizens have already figned the general Addrefs, which was projected, prepared, and figned in the fhort Space of thirty Hours, and prefented to you on the Morning of your Departure, with the Signature of near three hundred of the principal Perfons of the Settlement, to which large Additions have been fince made, and ftill are making.

But it was judged, that an Addrefs from the Officers of the Army in their collective Capacity, after you had left the Settlement, would more fully demonftrate to yourfelf, and to all the World, how very dear you were to them as Soldiers, and afford them an Opportunity of recording the Caufes of their Efteem, by a Recital of the Events which produced it.

We all know, Sir, either by having feen it, or by having heard it from thofe who were on the Spot, that you have been very near thirteen Years at the Head of this Settlement: That you came to the Chair as Governor immediately after the moft dreadful Calamity that ever befel a People, and found the Country much depopulated, the Treafury empty, and a moft

enormous

enormous Debt contracted: That the Plans
which you fo judicioufly laid when Governor,
were afterwards carried into Execution by the
Governor General and Supreme Council, of
which you have hitherto been the Head, and
effected a Difcharge of the Debt, filled the
Treafury with Cafh, and reftored Life and Vigour to the Country: That during this Period,
the Government was convulfed by jarring In-
terefts and unufual Oppofition; but, neverthe-
lefs, you maintained your Poft with Dignity
to the State, with Honour to yourfelf, and Con-
fufion to the Enemies of our Country: That
the Natives, taking advantage of what they
fuppofed a divided Government, entered into
a Confederacy to deftroy the Influence of the
Englifh in India, and to fet up that of the
French, who fecretly promoted the Union, and
afterward joined in League with them: That
all thefe Efforts were baffled, and India preferved to us, by your Firmnefs and the Vigour
of your Government, from which an Expe-
dition planned by yourfelf was fent forth, and
an Army under General Goddard traverfed
Regions unknown from the Eaft to the Weft
of India, and, in fpite of the Difafters which
befel thofe who were to co-operate, reached the
Coafts of Surat, and conquered Provinces
from the Powers at War with our Nation.

It is alfo well known, that in the midft of
this Scene of Trouble, the French and Spa-
niards, and afterwards the Dutch, joined to attack us, and were aided by the late Hyder
Allee, who, before the Dutch War, invaded

the

the Carnatic, defeated the Englifh in Battle, and reduced to his Obedience the whole of that Country, except Madras and Vellore, and fome few paltry Forts in the Neighbourhood of the Prefidency: That when all Men confidered the State of the Carnatic to be defperate, you rofe to refcue them from impending Ruin; and though Bengal was threatened with Invafions, nobly refolving to meet the Enemy at a Dif-tance, you fent out two Detachments, which gave Strength and Vigour to the Army under Sir Eyre Coote, thereby faved the Britifh Pof-feffions in that Part of India, and reduced the Enemy to conclude an honourable Peace with-out the fmalleft Lofs of Territory; and laftly, that the Armies ferving at a Diftance were paid, fed, clothed, and armed, by the Exertions and Refources of your Government.

Thus, Sir, under your Adminiftration, have the united Efforts of our numerous and power-ful Enemies been fruftrated; and India, by the Conquefts there made from the European Powers, has afforded the Means of redeeming what the Nation loft to them in every other Part of the Globe.

We therefore entreat you to accept this juft and grateful Tribute of our Praifes, and our warmeft Thanks for having opened the Paths which led to Glory, and afforded to the Bengal Army the Means of acquiring Honour, and of being ferviceable to the State at large.

Permit us now, Sir, to exprefs our Feelings on your Departure. Time, and the Contem-

plation

plation of your illustrious Actions, created an Esteem which is deeply rooted in our Hearts; and our Sorrow at losing the Man whom we considered as the Father of the Settlement, is, as it ought to be, great and poignant; we must therefore seek for Consolation in our Hopes, that you are going to receive those Honours and Rewards which are due to superior Merit; and with united Voice we pray that such may be the Event.

Signed by   4 Colonels,
             15 Lieutenant Colonels,
             25 Majors,
             71 Captains,
          324 Lieutenants,
            47 Ensigns,
            71 Lieut. Fire Workers, Surgeons,
                  &c. &c.

Total   557

THANKS

FROM THE

PROPRIETORS and DIRECTORS of
the EAST INDIA COMPANY.

IN the Month of December 1782, the Court of Proprietors, by a Majority of near [?] to one, returned Mr. Hastings their Thanks for his Services, and in particular, for his Exertions during the War in support of the Carnatic and Bombay.

In the Month of November 1783, the Court of Proprietors again returned their Thanks to Mr. Hastings for his Services; and in particular, for having effected a Peace with the Marattas.

In March 1784, the Court of Directors expressed, in the strongest Terms, their Sense of the Services performed by Mr. Hastings, in furnishing [?] the Support of the War.

In December 1784, the Thanks of the Proprietors were transmitted to Mr. Hastings, with the following Resolution of the Court of Directors:

THANKS

FROM THE

PROPRIETORS *and* DIRECTORS *of* *the* EAST INDIA COMPANY.

————————

IN the Month of October 1782, the Court of Proprietors, by a Majority of near six to one, returned Mr. Haftings their Thanks for his Services, and in particular for his Exertions during the War, in fupport of the Carnatic and Bombay.

In the Month of November 1783, the Court of Proprietors again returned their Thanks to Mr. Haftings for his Services; and in particular, for having effected a Peace with the Marattas.

In March 1784, the Court of Directors expreffed, in the ftrongeft Terms, their Senfe of the Services performed by Mr. Haftings, *in furnifhing Supplies* for the Support of the War.

In December 1784, the Thanks of the Proprietors were tranfmitted to Mr. Haftings, with the following Refolution of the Court of Directors:

rectors: " As Peace and Tranquillity are now
" perfectly eftablifhed throughout India, and
" this Court being fenfible that this happy Event
" has been principally owing to the very able,
'" and fpirited Exertions of our Governor Ge-
" neral, and the Supreme Council:

" Refolved unanimoufly, That the Thanks
" of this Court be conveyed to Warren Haftings
" Efquire, for his firm, unwearied, and fuccefs-
" ful Endeavours, in procuring the late Peace
" with the feveral Powers in India."

In February 1785, they expreffed their ftrong
and unanimous Senfe *of the long, faithful, and
able Services of Mr. Haftings.*

In June 1785, Mr. Haftings, on his Arrival
in England, was introduced to the Court of
Directors; when the Chairman, by Order, and
in the Name of the Court, returned him their
unanimous Thanks for the long, faithful, and
able Services which he had rendered the Eaft
India Company.

CON.

CONTENTS.

INTRODUCTORY PAPERS.

Z   AD-

CONTENTS.

ADDRESSES.

CONTENTS.

Z 2

CONTENTS.

CONTENTS.

CALCUTTA.

CONTENTS.

THE END.

This Day is Published,

In One large Volume Octavo, containing near One Thoufand Pages,
Price 10s. 6d.

THE

H I S T O R Y

AND

P R O C E E D I N G S

OF THE

LORDS AND COMMONS

OF

GREAT BRITAIN,

IN PARLIAMENT;

WITH REGARD TO THE REGENCY,

CONTAINING

A Full Account of all their Speeches on the propofed REGENCY
BILL, from November 20, 1788, to March 10, 1789, when HIS
MAJESTY's happy Recovery took place, and put a ftop to all farther
Proceedings on that Subject.

To which are added,

The THREE REPORTS of the PHYSICIANS;

Mr. PITT's LETTER to the PRINCE of WALES,

With HIS ROYAL HIGHNESS's ANSWER:

The REGENCY BILL, as it paffed the HOUSE OF COMMONS,
and was carried to the LORDS, and there read a Second Time;

AND

The Speeches of the LORDS and COMMONS OF IRELAND,
on appointing the PRINCE OF WALES REGENT WITHOUT
RESTRICTIONS; with a Copy of their ADDRESS, and the
PRINCE's ANSWER.

Printed for JOHN STOCKDALE.

ALSO,

A COLLECTION OF TRACTS

ON THE PROPOSED

R E G E N C Y,

In Two large Volumes Octavo, Price 1l. 10s.

SHAKSPEARE, with ·a Complete INDEX.

In the Prefs, and fpeedily will be publifhed,

In One large Volume Octavo, containing near 1400 Pages,

Printed upon a fine Royal Paper, and embellifhed with a
Head of the Author,

SHAKSPEARE,

INCLUDING,

IN ONE VOLUME,

The Whole of his Dramatic Works;

WITH

EXPLANATORY NOTES,

COMPILED FROM VARIOUS COMMENTATORS.

To which will be now firft added,

A copious Index to all the remarkable Paffages and
Words,

Calculated to point out the different Meanings in which the Words are
made ufe of by Shakfpeare:

By the Rev. SAMUEL AYSCOUGH, F. A. S.
And Affiftant Librarian of the Britifh Mufeum.

LONDON:
Printed for JOHN STOCKDALE, Piccadilly.

☞ The want of an Index to all the beautiful and remarkable Paffages
in Shakfpeare has long been regretted, but the difficulty of the under-
taking has hitherto prevented every attempt. Mr. Stockdale has already experienced a liberal encouragement from the Public for his Edition of Shakfpeare, in one Volume 8vo. and to whom he begs leave to
return his grateful acknowledgments. As the prefent edition will
coft him near £. 2000, he humbly folicits the affiftance of the ad-
mirers of Shakfpeare, by favouring him with their names as fub-
fcribers.
*A lift of the encouragers of a work which is intended to make this favourite
author ftill more ufeful and agreeable, will be prefixed.*
The price will not exceed *One Guinea*; and payment will not be required
until the work is publifhed.